T0358160

good
friends
BRING
salad

ANITA CAMPBELL

Wakefield
Press

Wakefield Press
1 The Parade West
Kent Town
South Australia 5067
www.wakefieldpress.com.au

First published 2005 by Anita Campbell
Wakefield Press edition published 2005
Copyright © Anita Campbell, 2005

Designed and typeset by Leigh Warren
Back cover wedding photo by Carol Darby
Printed and bound by Hyde Park Press

ISBN 1 86254 696 7

Wakefield Press thanks Fox Creek Wines
for their support.

Government of South Australia

Arts SA

"There is no love sincerer than the love of food"
George Bernard Shaw (1903)

THE CHALLENGE

It was coming from behind me, whispers followed by laughter. Surely they weren't laughing at me, were they? I had kept well away from scandal that year and except for my 'protractor' eyes, I was sure I had no other obvious defects.

I couldn't make out what they were saying; then suddenly it became clear, they were calling me 'D.C.' What could that mean? The following days were very uncomfortable, I became increasingly paranoid, and as the joke began to spread and laughter filled the classroom, I even considered not going to school. Eventually one of the boys felt so sorry for me that he told me what it meant. Get ready for it, the moment that changed my life, the moment that shaped the next ten years. D.C. meant double chin! My life was over.

I am sure most people, have similar horror stories from their school years, and I admit that on occasion I may have been the instigator. For that I am sorry. But, until that day I was unaware I even had a weight problem and had hardly any insecurities about myself. Of course, looking back now, I realise I wasn't overweight at all; I was just developing like a pubescent teenager should.

I sit here today wishing that I could be a size 10 again, and wondering why on earth I kept on gaining weight after that moment? Logic suggests that I would have been shocked into losing weight, and been so traumatised by the incident that I would make sure I was never a target for name calling ever again. Unfortunately, this was not the case; I initially lost a few kilos, but after high school I went down hill, big time!

The truth is, since the D.C. incident I have been burdened with the laughter and taunts of my peers and carry it around with me every day. I have had enough! I am sick and tired of feeling as though I am still being laughed at. I can't even go out for the night without agonising over whether or not people are disgusted by me.

It ends now! I have been on many diets in my short lifetime and I continue to put the weight right back on. I have decided that I am going to make up my own diet. I basically plan to watch my food intake and increase my activity levels, I am going to change my lifestyle so that I will get to a level which I can comfortably maintain. No more of these "seven-day" diets or "counting points" diets, I have had enough. I just want to be comfortable!

I sit here tonight feeling fat and ugly. I currently weigh 94.8kgs; I am 170cms tall and 26 years old. My goal is to lose 25 kilos in six months, approximately four kilos per month (or 0.14kgs per day at 182 days, if you are as anal as me); this will definitely be a challenge but a do-able one.

I recently went to my doctor, rather than the latest women's magazine; I figure he probably knows more about weight loss and sustainability. First up he described me as "obese", I was shocked, what a horrible word!! To make things worse, instead of offering me the miracle pill I was hoping for, he suggested I try exercise, wow! Who would have thought?

So I have hired a cross training machine, and purchased a set of electronic scales. I have eaten all the fattening food in the house and am ready to take on the world!

I thought I would bring you along on my quest for thinness and self-discovery. I hope that by the end of this journey I will have learnt that there is more to life than shopping at 1626 and deciding which flavour milk shake to get.

I will wake up tomorrow, Saturday, please don't start on a Monday let's change things up a bit, I will avoid foods which I know I shouldn't eat, exercise at least half an hour each day and drink at least one litre of water a day, the rest I will let you know as we go.

If you are game, join me. I suggest you keep a journal much like this one, who knows you may be famous one day! I also recommend that you take a before photo, make sure it is extra gross so you can put it on your fridge to remind yourself how disgusting you feel, this will also come in handy when you sell your story to *That's Life*.

Good night, I am going to have something bad for dessert, feel sick and frumpy and then wake up a new woman, well in the mind at least…for now!

This is the last time I am going to start a diet!

Bring it on!

DAY ONE

I started off well today, reducing my toast to two slices instead of three. I then had a low fat hot chocolate and a very small piece of jam roll for morning tea. My sister came over for lunch, luckily she knows about my diet and brought healthy food. My sister and I are very good at keeping each other fat! I had a low fat ham roll, minus the salad, and some rice crackers, minus the taste. We then decided to bake some low fat muffins and of course they had to be taste tested, Yum! Hint: Buy the cake mix which is low fat but still has icing, you can divide it up in a muffin tin, which guarantees twelve portions and each one gets icing, much more inviting!

We walked to the park, and the kids played for a while, and then we came home, probably a total length of 20 minutes walking. I have not yet had a sip of water, and I am probably bordering on clinical dehydration. I will try to rectify my water intake this evening when I do my exercise and, I will also have water with dinner. Furthermore today, I have not yet had a single piece of fruit or vegetable, and probably won't – well maybe a mandarin.

As you can see my idea of a diet is probably Jennifer Aniston's idea of a binge. Oh well it just means I have more time to ease myself into my new lifestyle.

Unfortunately I am not much of a vegetable fan and don't like many fruits; so when I start eating like a rabbit it will probably mean I have turned into one!

I have decided that since all the celebrities are going on these low carb (carbohydrate) diets, I might give it a try; tomorrow I will not eat carbs after 6pm, like I said I am easing myself in. After 6pm I will only eat protein, I love cheese, so cheese it is! This diet is going to be great!

DAY TWO

Ok I am not allowed any more carbs today, this will be a mission, because I am used to having lots, especially around 8pm. Today went well and I am extra proud of myself for succeeding in the face of adversity, I had a chocolate biscuit in my hand and did not eat it. They were treats for the kids, not me. I am hoping that this journey will help me to mature; I still like to have treats and hot chips with the kids at the shops. I also enjoy and expect something sweet after dinner. I am especially bad at kids' parties; give me fairy bread and little boys any day!

Today an elderly relative of mine so graciously mentioned that I was finally starting to look attractive??? What do you say to that…well thanks Love; I do feel much less like an ugly pig. There I go again, I am so negative… At least she noticed…

Ok back to the food, it's always about the food? I feel as if my whole life revolves around what I am going to eat next. As a child I would only sleep at friends houses if I knew they had yummy dinners, which was very rare. On a number of occasions I was still sitting at the table hours after dinner was served, I remember the two hour spaghetti bolognaise incident vividly. I had many friends keen to sleep at my house though, I wonder if it was because of the 99% chance of take-away.

I don't know why, but I am very fussy; it is something I have battled with since childhood. If you are thinking yes you too are fussy, please read this list of my pet hates, if anyone can beat my fussiness I want to meet you, perhaps we could start a self-help group "Fussy Eaters Anonymous".

Here goes. I don't like:

- Sauce, any type, yes even on hotdogs
- Pizza, not even Hawaiian
- Mayonnaise, coleslaw, potato salad or sour cream
- Red meat, not for political reasons I just can't eat it
- Most fruit; bananas, strawberries, mango, peaches etc
- Most veggies except peas, corn, carrot, cucumber and lettuce
- Coffee or Tea, I am a Milo girl
- Pasta or noodles, well I like egg noodles
- Holey, smelly or melted cheeses
- Hamburgers, I've never had one, I wouldn't like it though
- Anything involving cream and fruit
- Seafood of any type
- Custard
- Most stuff from the bakery except hedgehog slice
- Meat Pies and/or mince, including tacos
- Yogurt and anything made from bacteria

I am sure there are more but that's enough to convince you that I am a complete nutter. I promise you except for my food problems I really am quite sane, why else would I be telling all my intimate secrets to the world.

Basically you can see I have spent the last twenty odd years living off carbohydrates. During the next six months I aim to increase the variety of food that I eat and try at least ten new foods. I will keep you posted. Last night I had a bowl of low fat oven fries for tea, I know not good, tonight I added chicken, and I will add veggies tomorrow night.

I managed 20 minutes on the cross trainer last night, pretty impressive! Considering I could only do two minutes at a time when I first got it. Trust me it does get easier!! I will try for 25 minutes tonight. I think it is important to keep your goals achievable and within reach. Lots of small successes are better than one big fat failure. It is the little achievements that help to get you to the main goal! Look at Paris Hilton and Pamela Anderson; they both had success in small films before they became "Mega Stars". And your goals don't have to be about your weight, it is good to have other ambitions that can help to take your mind off food.

Currently my distractions are plenty, two beautiful boys Logan aged three and Alexander aged one, and a full time nursing degree. You may think this is a lot, considering my husband works two weeks on and one week off at a mine near Kalgoorlie, but I like to be busy. So far these distractions have not helped me to lose weight though, they have just given me great excuses to eat take-away food.

It took me seven years and five faculties to decide I want to be a Nurse. I started a Bachelor of Nursing at the beginning of 2003. Alexander was born in midsemester break and I went back when he was two weeks old. This was quite nice because two days per week I got a bit of a rest, he stayed with his Daddy, who was also studying at the time. All the other students complain about studying but to me it is a holiday!

Anyway, of course at university they sell muffins and chocolate milk, which I just have to buy, because I had no time to prepare real food. I aim to make more of an effort from now on, lots of the students have kids and they manage to bring healthy lunches, I can do it too!

DAY THREE

Ok, last night was a disaster, I did not exercise and I ate half a packet of lollies. Rule number one: do not have food in your house that can make you fat! Today I had cereal for breakfast; and at 11am I felt something I have not felt for a long time…hunger. This is a good thing. I was out at the shops at the time and amazingly enough I did not get hot chips, instead I chose a savoury scroll from the bakery, they have around 5 grams of fat and satisfy me quite nicely.

Subsequently I had to wash this down with something; I should have had a Diet Coke (or water). Instead I chose a low fat milk shake, which the shop assistant assured me, was skim milk and low fat ice cream. After one sip I believed him.

I also bought some low fat bread they call it low GI (glycemic index), which means that the energy lasts for longer and it doesn't turn into fat as easily, I think. Well it seems to be the fashion anyway, so at 3pm when I felt hungry again I had a vegemite sandwich, it filled me up.

So what is glycemic index all about??? I do a lot of work on the computer for uni and have found researching to be very easy on the internet. For the purpose of this book I am only going to include information that is freely available to everyone on the World Wide Web. Here's what I found out about G.I:

"The glycemic index is a ranking of carbohydrates based on their immediate effect on blood glucose (blood sugar) levels. It compares foods gram for gram of carbohydrate. Carbohydrates that breakdown quickly during digestion have the highest glycemic indexes. The blood glucose response is fast and high. Carbohydrates that break down slowly, releasing glucose gradually into the blood stream, have low glycemic indexes."

It is claimed that[1]:

- *Low GI means a smaller rise in blood glucose levels after meals*
- *Low GI diets can help people lose weight*
- *Low GI diets can improve the body's sensitivity to insulin*
- *High GI foods help re-fuel carbohydrate stores after exercise*
- *Low GI can improve diabetes control*
- *Low GI foods keep you fuller for longer*
- *Low GI can prolong physical endurance*

To me this low GI thing just seems like another diet fad, so I kept searching.

Choice Magazine state that:

"The suggestion that low-GI diets can help us lose weight and keep it off is based on the argument that the faster we digest our food, the sooner we're hungry again

and the more we tend to eat. While this seems plausible, there's in fact little evidence to support the idea.[2]"

I have given up on the no carbs thing too; I saw a show on television today, which said that you should always accompany protein with carbs. They also said that you should eat lots of fruit and vegetables, I know, I know, I will I promise.

I must say I am very proud of myself though; I have not had anything deep-fried for three days! This has got to be a record! I aim to have take-away food only when my husband is home from work. When he comes home he likes to have take-away a couple of times, and even then I will try to choose the low fat options.

I tried on a pair of size 18 jeans today, a good wake up call. I don't know who would have worn them because, if they had done up, they would have shown my butt crack. I really hate it when they try to make modern clothes for over weight people, they don't actually make them fit well, they just increase the size of the waist. Not all of us fatties want to look like Britney Spears!!! I ended up buying a pair from Jeans West they had an excellent selection of jeans going up to size 20, lots of different styles, it made me feel like a normal person!

I have to exercise extra tonight, I really am not looking forward to it, I am so lazy that the thought of having to change into exercise clothes, then shower and wash my hair is all a bit too much. But it must be done! Good night…

DAY FOUR

Last night I managed 20 minutes on the cross trainer. I had a great day, I started off by weighing myself first thing, just before I got into the shower, I was 93.6kgs. I know the difference between night and morning has contributed to the loss but it still feels great to see a reduction. I will weigh myself once every three days at the same time from now on. I am too impatient to wait a week!

I had cereal with low fat milk for breakfast and I discovered Subway!! I didn't have any morning tea today so at 1.30pm my sister and I got Subway, it was my very first foot long, I had a ham one with no cheese or sauce, and boy did it fill me up. According to their packaging this was approx 9 grams of fat. I had a cookie for a treat and a bottle of diet coke. I have had no other snacks today and feel very satisfied! I have also forgotten to mention that I have stuck to my one litre of water per day, which is great, however I feel like I am getting up at night more than a pregnant woman does... we must make sacrifices!

I had salad in my roll, but still no fruit, I will try tonight...

DAY FIVE

Last night went well; I did not exercise because it took three hours to get my temperamental three-year old to sleep. I had a multigrain sandwich for dinner and for dessert I had low fat chocolate mousse.

People; don't get fooled by marketing, always read your labels! I went to the supermarket to buy a low fat dessert today, I found the section with all the low fat ticks and points; the huge range and variety surprised me. I checked them all out and decided on low-fat mousse; I then spotted another chocolate mousse, much more inviting, the packaging looked much more like a treat and guess what, it appears to be the exact same product, they are even made by the same people, I would say this is a case of customer manipulation. The same product has been marketed for dieters and for non-dieters. This doesn't bother me but it does make me wonder… I will keep you posted on any others super market marvels I discover.

Well like I said I am impatient, who wants to wait one whole week to find out that they have only lost 0.1kgs, even though a loss is a loss it is not very motivating. So of course I got on the scales this morning. I am so pumped; I weighed 93.4kgs, that's 0.2kg loss since yesterday, that's one of the packets of chocolate biscuits gone.

I have now officially changed to low fat foods, I now have reduced fat milk, ice cream, desserts, biscuits and margarine, and have switched to whole meal or multigrain bread, it may not be lower in fat but is higher in fibre. I have become aware of the fibre content in foods because I heard on TV that it is best to eat foods with at least 3gms of fibre per 100gms. So my cereal this morning was fine, accompanied with low fat milk and no extra spoons of sugar it was a very satisfying breakfast.

DAY SIX

Last night was great, I had the kids under control by 7.45 pm so I got on the cross trainer and did 25 minutes, watching the Olympics whist exercising certainly helps. I probably could have done more but then I will make it hard to keep improving. Slow and steady wins the race… that is my new motto; I don't want to put this weight back on again, ever! I weighed 93.2kgs this morning and feel great. I had Subway again for lunch; maybe I can do an advert for them when my book is published.

I also discovered Darrell Lea chocolate bars. As usual I felt like something sweet after my lunch so I bought a Caramel Snow bar, it has 7 grams of fat, which is around half the amount of normal chocolate bars. In future this will be a real treat for me because the fat content is still a bit too high. They also sell nougat bars which are covered in chocolate and contain even less fat, I will try one tomorrow and let you know if they are worthy.

I really should stop calling this a diet, I have always thought of a diet as something that was going to end but I don't intend for this new eating plan to end. I will slowly incorporate healthier foods and increased exercise until I reach a comfortable level, one that could be maintained for the rest of my life.

I do not recommend quick fix diets, which require you to completely change your eating habits and make life very uncomfortable. That sort of diet has kept me yo-yoing for the past five years.

I can't wait until I can buy clothes from any shop and not feel as though I am being stared at when I walk around in public. Especially when I eat in public, I always feel as though people are looking and thinking, well no wonder she's fat. It's funny because if you saw an attractive thin woman eating McDonalds you wouldn't even look twice, but a fat person is "disgusting". I can't wait to be thin!!!

DAY SEVEN

Last night I only used the cross trainer for 15 minutes, for some reason it has started to get very squeaky, I can't use it like this because I will wake up the kids and risk breaking it. I will ring the hire company this afternoon to see what's wrong. This morning I weighed 93.0kgs this is a steady loss of 0.2kgs per day. Please don't be disheartened if you don't lose straight away because when you start increasing your fluid intake your body's cells become fuller, this can increase your weight initially. Don't worry it will benefit you later!!!

Ok today I figured I would need to start adding some facts about obesity and nutrition to this book it is reassuring to know that I am not the only fat person out there. By the way if you think I use the word fat a lot, it is because that is how I feel, fat and ugly. Not over weight, that's too nice a phase and not obese because that is just wrong. All information below was found at the World Health Organisation's (W.H.O.) web page; it has lots of interesting information.

Obesity and Overweight[3]

"Obesity and overweight pose a major risk for serious diet-related chronic diseases, including type 2 diabetes, cardiovascular disease, hypertension and stroke, and

certain forms of cancer. The health consequences range from increased risk of premature death, to serious chronic conditions that reduce the overall quality of life.

As incomes rise and populations become more urban, diets high in complex carbohydrates give way to more varied diets with a higher proportion of fats, saturated fats and sugars. At the same time, large shifts towards less physically demanding work have been observed worldwide. Moves towards less physical activity are also found in the increasing use of automated transport, technology in the home, and more passive leisure pursuits.

The prevalence of overweight and obesity is commonly assessed by using body mass index (BMI), defined as the weight in kilograms divided by the square of the height in metres (kg/m^2). A BMI over 25 kg/m^2 is defined as overweight, and a BMI of over 30 kg/m^2 as obese.

The more life-threatening problems fall into four main areas: CVD problems; conditions associated with insulin resistance such as type 2 diabetes; certain types of cancers, especially the hormonally related and large-bowel cancers; and gallbladder disease. The likelihood of developing Type 2 diabetes and hypertension rises steeply with increasing body fatness. Confined to older adults for most of the 20th century, this disease now affects obese children even before puberty. Approximately 85% of people with diabetes are type 2, and of these, 90% are obese or overweight.

Raised BMI also increases the risks of cancer of the breast, colon, prostrate, endometrium, kidney and gallbladder.

What can we do about it?

Promoting healthy behaviours to encourage, motivate and enable individuals to lose weight by:

- *eating more fruit and vegetables, as well as nuts and whole grains;*
- *engaging in daily moderate physical activity for at least 30 minutes;*
- *cutting the amount of fatty, sugary foods in the diet;*
- *moving from saturated animal-based fats to unsaturated vegetable-oil based fats"*

I have calculated my current Body Mass Index (BMI) at 32.2

> Calculation:
> Your height in meters multiplied by itself, gives you the square, so:
>
> 1.7 x 1.7 = 2.89
>
> Now divide your weight by the figure above so:
>
> 93.0 (2.89 = 32.1799

…this means according to the W.H.O., I am obese (my doctor was right). So for me to reduce my BMI to 24, which is just below the overweight zone…

Calculation:
Your height squared multiplied by the BMI which you want, so:

2.89 x 24 = 69.36

...I need to weigh 69kgs. I was pretty close with a goal of 70kgs! I will adjust my goal to 69kgs.

DAY EIGHT

OK last night, no exercise, the same excuse, squeaky machine. Apparently I need to oil it, I will get some today. I weighed in at 92.4kgs, yes... a great loss!!! This takes my total to 2.4kgs in a little over a week. That is good, and very motivating. However I would not want to keep this up, my doctor informed me that rapid weight loss is not as permanent and you are much more likely to gain it back again. I am sure I will begin to slow down soon, it is just the lack of saturated fats that is making the difference, and oh yeah eight days without deep-fried, do I get a gold star?

I figured now that you know all the ins and outs of overweight and obesity, you need some guidelines to healthy eating from the Better Health Channel, this may clear up all those "chocolate is good for you" myths:

<u>Healthy Diets for All Australians</u>[4] In general, we should all eat:

- *Low salt foods and use salt sparingly*
- *A wide variety of nutritious foods*
- *Plenty of breads and cereals (particularly wholegrain), vegetables, legumes (such as chickpeas) and fruit*

- *Only moderate amounts of foods containing sugars.*
- *A healthy diet can also include a limited intake of alcohol*
- *A good balance between exercise and food intake is important; this helps to maintain a healthy body weight.*
- *Keep dietary fat to a minimum*
- *Be sure to eat foods which contain calcium and iron*

I'm sure you have all seen a food pyramid before basically we all know what is bad for us don't we... And while we are on the topic of chocolate, the nougat bars from Darrell Lea are lovely!

DAY NINE

Today I weighed in at 92.2kgs I am so amped!!! This helps to make up for my disastrous day yesterday. I have never done this before and it must be because I am getting too thin. I cried at the shops. OK I was a blubbering mess, all because the guy at the optometrist wouldn't give me my contact lenses until I paid $130, despite the fact that I was told they would be totally covered by my health fund and I would only need to pay $30 for the appointment. I think what did it was the fact that I had the contact lens attached to my eyes, and I was going to have to take them out and give them back, I felt like a common criminal.

Anyway I did learn something from this, if you cry you get what you want. The shop assistant wrapped it all up for me and very nicely told me to leave; we could sort it out on Monday. I was shocked when I left the store; I am not usually an overly emotional person. I have come to the conclusion that as I am now thin (well near enough) I must be getting weaker; this explains the actresses who cry when they receive awards. Luckily I am not an aspiring actress; I wouldn't even be able to get down the red carpet. And yes, now I have contacts, for the first time. They make me feel more attractive and highlight my lovely green eyes.

Again no exercise, I need to get some oil. Ok I am not being lazy, I promise! Here is some important information on nutritional labels to help put you to sleep.

I have developed this quick guide from info found on the Woolworths web site,[5]:

- Firstly, the ingredients must be listed in descending order of weight in the product – the major ingredient comes first. So if sugar is the first ingredient, and it is a breakfast cereal, it's probably not the best choice.
- *Food labels are not permitted to make claims that are false or misleading. But watch out for "lite" foods, this could mean they are light in colour, or even flavour.*
- *Labels are also not supposed to make health claims about foods. For example, a food label may not state that eating a particular food will prevent heart disease, bowel cancer or any other condition.*
- *No food may be labelled as being suitable for diabetics and none may be classified as being "slimming" or to have weight-reducing properties.*
- *Health authorities are working on precise definitions for terms such as 'natural' and for regulations governing what is 'low' or 'reduced' or 'high' in particular foods.*
- *Kilojoules/calories – Certain foods can be described as 'low joule' or 'low calorie' if a prescribed serving of the food has no more than 70kj (17 cals).*
- *Fats – Some foods now have laws governing claims for fat-reduced or low fat. For example, low-fat ice cream must not contain more than 4% fat (by*

weight); reduced-fat ice cream must not have more than 6.5% fat (by weight).

One of the most important things to look out for is the serving sizes, they often state that there is a certain amount of fat per serving. You are then led to believe that the whole packet contains that amount of fat. Wrong. Watch out they often use this to make the fat content look lower. This is especially important with desserts. You know those small tubs of Yogo, which they sell separately, apparently there are two servings in each tub, even my three year old would eat the tub in one sitting. This is also true for some flavoured milk, just be aware!

Also I looked up the word 'lite' in my dictionary, apparently there is no such word???

DAY TEN

Well, I bought some oil, but haven't had time to use it yet, so yes, another night gone. Anyway, yesterday ended up to be a life-changing day. I decided I could no longer handle being so poor that I resort to crying at the shops so I thought - why not sell the house, pay off debts and build again. I put a hold on a block 5mins east of where I live now and chose the house I wanted. You should know by now I don't do things in halves. Some call me erratic, I would say a little eccentric but otherwise very unstable...no, no, no...I am an Aquarian!

My poor husband is away and I am just changing our lives around, I can't understand why he is so speechless, I would be so excited. Well he did live in the same house for twenty-three years, and since meeting me we have lived in four...nearly five. Well stay tuned it will be fun, who knows I may even pose nude for Playboy.

I forgot to tell you that I had hot chips on Saturday night, and I didn't feel bad. I had a Subway 6inch and some chips to go with it. Probably $1/3$ the amount I would usually have and I didn't even clean up the kids plates, I didn't need to. Also I skipped dessert. This morning I weighed 92.0kgs. What can I say, this is much easier than I had imagined. I hope you are still with me… I want to read all your success stories, perhaps even publish a book full of successes.

DAY ELEVEN

I did 3.4kms on the cross trainer, and then it squeaked again, the oil is crap, I will phone them again tomorrow. This weight loss thing is very hard to organise; I can understand why people give up, but hey if Oprah Winfrey and Sarah Ferguson can't stick to it, how is any normal (poor) person going to?

My husband came home today, yay, it's great to feel so happy to see him. I think it brings spice back into our relationship, don't get me wrong we still talk on the phone once or twice a day while he's away but It's just nice to enjoy his company instead of having him in my face all day every day. It is also nice not to have to think of new excuses not to be intimate, especially at bedtime!

I have an exam on Friday, so I had better go to bed…yes I ate badly today but much better than the old bad…and I just played a game of netball too.

Good night.

DAY FOURTEEN

OK I have three words for you. FAT. DISGUSTING. PIG… I have been off track big time. But thankfully all the fatty food has made me feel ill. I got my period a few days ago and then I decided, what the hell, Jai is home I can eat what I want.

What is my problem…I am in denial; I can't eat what I want if I want to be thin. It is a fact of life. After my exam I went to the movies with a friend, I must say I only drank water but I had ice cream and popcorn. You may be thinking well that's not too bad, but this does not compare to the hot chips for tea and the Hungry Jacks for tea the night before, or even the packet of chippies the day before that. I was doing so well…

I am now back on track again…until tomorrow night, I am going to a quiz night. I forgot to tell you I am very competitive and love a good trivia night. Wish me luck, cos I really need more useless shit in my house!

By the way the house selling idea has been scrapped, my mum owns half the house and is not keen on the idea. We will refinance instead, once all our bills are paid, and we can actually get a loan from someone. Don't worry though I will have a new project soon.

DAY SIXTEEN

OK well I am still a disgusting, fat, pig and to tell you the truth I am sitting here eating biscuits while I type. I am eating because I am dealing with some emotional problems. People often call themselves "emotional eaters" but never really understand why. I believe we eat when we are emotional because it makes us feel secure, the taste is familiar and this makes us feel more comfortable, not to mention all those addictive chemicals added to get you hooked.

It is a long story, but for some reason my Mum has the ability to make me feel like a piece of crap! I do know that she doesn't mean to do it but at the moment my self-esteem is not too good. I think taking this journey is making me stronger; I am really getting to know myself. I don't mean to get all 'Dr Phil' on you but it doesn't hurt to look at why you are eating, when you are not hungry. For me chocolate makes me feel warm and fuzzy, it is my best friend!

I wonder how much I have gained?

DAY EIGHTEEN

I am writing this whilst my three year old cries himself to sleep, oh the joys of daytime sleeps at daycare! Well I have gained 0.2kgs, what a waste. This is usually the point at which I would give up and make various excuses as to why I should just stay fat. These reasons have often included the fact that I may get pregnant again and therefore the weight loss would be worthless. I have also convinced myself that being large is genetic and that if my mum is overweight then I should be too, plus I have always liked that 'big butts' song. These ridiculous excuses work well on the mind, but not on the body.

Ok I believe that family history does play a part in your weight, but I think it is more nurture than nature. It is the eating habits that you inherit not the actual weight. I am going to try to recognise this and be stricter with my eating this week. I am back on track with my water intake, boy I have noticed the difference, especially with my bowels (sorry I couldn't think of a nicer way to put it).

I have fixed the cross trainer and will start using it again tomorrow. I have made myself a small goal, and that is that if I lose a total of ten kilos by the 24th October (a month and a half away) I can go to Rock It, a rock concert held near my house. I need to achieve this because last time I went I must have been blind! I walked out of the house with a halter neck top on, have you seen the movie Shallow Hal? Well you get the picture then. This time I want to feel happy with my appearance and be more comfortable around strangers. So far I have lost 2.6 kilos so I have 7.4kgs to go…

DAY TWENTY

I am back in action, last night I used the cross trainer for twenty minutes and 4.3kms. It felt great, I really do enjoy exercise I just hate the preparation and then having to change clothes and shoes fifty times in one day, ok call me lazy, but it's a pain in the bum. Whilst I was on the cross trainer I was watching some of the fashion week on the news, good motivation, all those skinny things. Anyway one of the designers stated that she had swim suits to suit "everyone" they even went up to 'size sixteen', at this point I started moving faster. My god I am not part of "everyone", so what part am I????

That was the point where I am supposed to say; 'that is disgusting she should cater for all people even the fat ones', but hey who really wants to see a size 20 person in a bikini? I know I would not feel comfortable in one that's for sure. Even when I lose my weight I would still have to hide those unsightly stretch marks and the excess skin. I hope that I can get some of it removed, I might have to apply for one of those medical shows though, I hear it's not cheap. Maybe I could donate it for skin grafts? I will look into it.

The best news of all is that today I weighed 91.8kgs!!! And someone noticed. I wonder why it is that when someone asks if you have lost weight we don't say "yes I have been working hard and I have lost 3 kilos in three weeks" instead I said, "yes a little" as if I am embarrassed to be on a diet. Lets face it, if they noticed the weight loss then they are aware that you are overweight, it is not a secret, and we should be glad they noticed and embrace the encouragement. Next time I will!

In order for me to go to *Rock It* I need to weigh 84.8kgs, this is scary because it feels so far away, I feel like I could never get below 90kgs. I will though and I can!!!

DAY TWENTY THREE

I am in a bit of a rut today, I got on the scales this morning and I weighed 92.6kgs, then I moved them to another spot and weighed 91.6kgs, what a bastard!!! Maybe I will just have to be patient and start weighing myself less regularly, and keep the scales in exactly the same position.

I suppose the real test will be when I go to the doctors, because when I first saw the doctor I weighed 92kgs, this was a few months ago and he told me that his scales were a bit lighter than most. I know that my measurements are a better way of analysing my weight loss, a couple of months ago my sister and I took measurements at various parts of our bodies. The trick to this is to pick places that you will use every time for example, I have a mole on my arm; which I use as my anchor for my arm measurement. That way you get more accurate results.

Here are my results:

Body area	30 May 2004	Today, 12 September 2004
Neck	39.0	38.5
Chest	106.0	105.0
Waist	109.0	106.0
Hips	120.0	117.0
Thigh	63.0	61.5
Calf	40.0	39.5
Arm	38.0	37.5

This is not as good as I thought it would be, I am going to step up my healthy eating, today I will eat fruit! I will not eat deep-fried food for at least 10 days!! I will keep drinking lots of water!!!

Over the past few days I have been quite good, and have done a total of 5.6kms on the cross trainer. I had an exam on Friday, which made Thursday night useless for exercise, and the weekend is always pretty hectic. I did discover that after dinner when you have that desperate urge for sweetness, a small glass of diet soft drink really helps. Of course it is not the healthiest choice but, if you are used to having ice cream or chocolate, it is much better.

The other night I was watching a current affairs show about anorexia. They showed a young lady who had battled with the disorder and looked like she was going to beat it. I found myself relating to her. I know, not exactly, but the way she felt completely out of control and how every minute of her day revolved around her food intake and her body image was exactly the way I feel. I began to realise that people who overeat are very similar to those who under eat. I believe that it is very likely, just like for anorexics, that there are underlying psychological reasons for overeating. And no I am not making excuses for myself; I am simply saying that, you can't fix the problem until you know what causes it!

For me the battle is to take each day as it comes and to realise that if I am having a bad day, a chocolate bar will only make me feel worse tomorrow! It is easy for me to say that you have to take this a day at a time, but if you look at why you are over eating rather that what you are eating you might find it easier.

Remember to let people know that you are trying not to eat fatty or sugary foods, that way they can avoid offering them to you. There will always be the people, like my mother, who knows I am dieting but decides to bring over fish and chips for lunch anyway, don't ask me why? I have no clue; I am so weak in these situations!!! Why can't she bring me a ham and salad sandwich???

My new motto is

"When Others Bring Cake; Good Friends Bring Salad"

DAY TWENTY FIVE

I can't believe I am still on this diet!!! I am motivated and have my eye on the goal. You may be thinking that twenty-five days is not long, but for me it is a very long time, not even a whole month, but remember one year in diet years is equivalent to six!

I weighed 91.4kgs this morning and managed a whopping 30 minutes on the cross trainer last night. It wasn't even hard, I am starting to get quite fit and I have noticed I am not as breathless when I walk up stairs.

My husband, being the gentleman that he is, is trying to be supportive of my weight loss. Last night he offered to pay for a breast enlargement for me, if I lose 20kgs. What a wonderful husband, setting me goals! Maybe if he too continues to lose weight I could also reward him with an enlargement operation of some sort.

Jai weighed around 116kgs on the day of our wedding and since he has been working away, he has lost around 10kgs. He looks great and has heaps more energy.

DAY TWENTY EIGHT

Boy have I made some achievements in the last few days. Firstly, I ate an apple, and it was nice! I know this is terrible twenty-eight days without fruit, but it is true and I promised myself that if I was going to write this book I had to be honest.

I weighed myself this morning, guess what…I am 90.8kgs, that's four kilos in four weeks and I have not had to starve once!!! I feel great, I am more energized and less fixated on food than I have ever been in my life.

But wait for it…this is the biggest achievement of my diet so far…I turned down a king size chocolate bar today. And what is even better is that they were free and there was a whole box of them just staring at me. The box was telling me to "just take one, it won't hurt, come on it's free, you can't pass up that kind of bargain". But I did!!!

DAY THIRTY ONE

This week has been wonderful, I have been on clinical placement at a hospital, and have found dieting to be a lot easier when you don't actually have time to eat. I am used to making breakfast at eight and then trying to fill in the time until lunch, this is not the case if you work as a nurse!

I used to have an office job, and although I was quite busy, I still found time to ring a co-worker, walk to the shop together, and eat at my desk, especially around three pm. There were also lots of lunches and special going away morning teas I had to try to avoid. I don't know what advice to give to those people who are continuously surrounded by food all day, except that perhaps you should become a nurse! Not only do you not have time for food, but with what you are exposed to during your shift, you probably wouldn't want to face food anyway.

I learnt today that an easy way to drink extra water is to have a glass before you drink any other type of drink. For example, today I felt thirsty so instead of just pouring a glass of Diet Coke, I had a glass of water first. I felt replenished and the coke became more of a pleasure than a thirst quencher. The extra water also helps to combat the negative action of the caffeine.

This morning I weighed 90.6kgs, I have not used the cross trainer very much this week because I have been so active at the hospital and have walked to the park twice in the last two days. This is a positive, because I don't intend to rent an exercise machine for the rest of my life, I am using it as a boost to my exercise levels and so I have no excuse not to use it. Eventually I will incorporate a high level of activity into my every day routine.

DAY FORTY

Well I have had a little diet holiday, lately. I have been off the rails big time. I had take-away three times last week and a block of chocolate. One thing that has been a positive is that not once was I satisfied by my binges, I feel this is a breakthrough!!! I was too scared to weigh myself last week, but today I realised I am not going to quit! I weighed 90.6kgs. Wow, that is not so bad, but I have just lost nine days? What am I thinking, she'll be right I will magically lose my weight in my sleep on day one hundred and eighty. It is time to get serious!

I have had a great day; here is what I have eaten:

Breakfast: Two slices of toast with peanut butter and vegemite

Hint: My peanut butter actually has less fat than my margarine. Please don't knock it till you have tried it, sweet and savoury in one, you can't lose

Lunch: Ham and Salad sandwich

Snacks: Around $1/3$ packet of Rice Crackers
An apple (I am proud, and they actually do taste nice)
2 very dry plain wheat biscuits

Dinner: 2 rashers of bacon grilled
1 omelette made up using 1 egg and a

splash of milk

(This was an accomplishment; I have not eaten an egg for many years. It is also a very low carb dinner, and I am not even hungry yet)

Dessert: Low fat hot chocolate sachet, I added some low fat milk

I have exercised tonight for 35 minutes; I think this is a record! I plan to start doing aerobics tomorrow morning…don't quote me on that.

Well good night for now, I hope you can stay on track; it will be worth it in the end. Remember looking better than that bitch at work has got to be worth more than a million chocolate bars!!!

DAY FORTY ONE

Wow I have done so well today, it seems that when I am completely focused I have no trouble eating well. I don't get cravings for chocolate or deep fried food, and I am certainly not starving. It is amazing to look at the amount of food I ate today, compared with what I used to eat; I could have fed a whole village just with my evening snacks!

Tonight I had my favourite food for dinner:

Home made wedges…very yummy!

Recipe:

Take one medium-large potato and cut it up into about 12 wedges (leave the skin on), then I boiled it in the microwave, then onto an oven tray and sprayed with cooking oil (the one in the aerosol, low fat), then sprinkle some all purpose seasoning on them, put into oven for as long as it takes to look cooked, then put them in a bowl so you feel like you are at an expensive café… enjoy!

During my evening soapies I managed 30 minutes on cross trainer and a record of 6.6kms. This is so exciting because I feel I have more energy, I know you have heard it before, but it's true, 30 minutes exercise gives me more energy than a chocolate bar.

One of my pet excuses for not losing weight is the "it costs too much to lose weight and eat well", this has now gone out the window. I can no longer use this excuse. Ok the low fat foods are often more expensive but have you added up the cost of three take-away dinners, muffins and coffees at work, ice creams and treats for dessert, and lets not forget those bloody vending machines!

I am now an advocate of not only losing weight but also saving money. In the past few days my total meal costs have been far less than a few months ago and I have even stopped buying the kids treats. They don't need them!!! All they need is a hug, and sometimes a quick kick up the butt...only joking, that's right "time out" is all the rage (for punishment) now, I wonder what underlying psychological issues that one is going to cause our young ones?

Getting back to business though, I am seriously considering, personally asking John Howard to open up clinics for people who need help to lose weight. Why should we have to pay thousands of dollars when the anorexics get their treatment for free? That may sound harsh but don't forget that heart disease is the biggest killer in Australians these days!

The Facts[6]:

- *Cardiovascular disease (CVD) is the term used for heart, stroke and blood vessel diseases and is the leading cause of death in Australia, accounting for 38% of all deaths in 2002; claiming the lives of more than one in three Australians.*

- *Risk factors for Cardiovascular disease include people who are overweight, relatively inactive, smoke daily, have diabetes, have high blood pressure and/ or high cholesterol*

- *60% of Australians are overweight – 7.42 million adults*

Surely the government can see that by implementing some sort of government-funded program to assist overweight people, they would ultimately cut their associated health care costs and therefore save money. It's probably not as easy as this, but it seems to be extremely hard for overweight people to get assistance, it is almost as though you need to be overly obese before you are considered to have a medical problem, why is this???

Oh yeah, I didn't do aerobics this morning, it was a bit unrealistic of me to think I would get up at 6.00am just to do exercise, maybe next year, or maybe never. If only I had a wake up call from my mate Johnny...

DAY FORTY TWO

I am at a loss for words tonight, I am very stressed out about my three year old. Ever since he was born (an horrendous 19 hour birth, very difficult on myself and even more difficult on him) he has been very temperamental. He has the ability to cry over very unimportant things, for example, tonight I did not give him the correct Spiderman drink bottle, so he cried and winged for hours.

He also has a lot of trouble relaxing and finds it very difficult to fall asleep. I have been back and forward to the paediatrician with him since he was six months old. No one can really explain why he is so temperamental. He has always had this inability to express emotions or he overly expresses emotions. Consequently I am always reluctant to do things that I feel might set him off, exercise is a good example. I used to say that I couldn't go out for walks with him because we would be out for five minutes then he would cry and scream until I got him out of the pram, perhaps if I had just bitten the bullet he would not be so fragile now.

For the past four years I have used my son's unpredictability as an excuse for not losing my post baby weight, all twenty-four kilos of it. I was 86 kilos when I got pregnant with Logan and weighed 110 kilos on the day of his birth.

I was reminded of this today when I went for a walk with both kids around my suburb. It went well, Alex (1yrs old) even fell asleep half way through which was nice because it meant Logan could play on the playground at the park. Well at least for five minutes until his pants got wet on the slide and he whinged until we got home. Otherwise it was a good day today, I ate well, and I weighed 90.2kgs this morning.

DAY FORTY FOUR

Well I did it…I have lost five kilos!

This morning I weighed 89.6kgs and I am wrapped. I have really been trying hard this week and it has paid off. I went to the Royal Show yesterday and only had hot chips, I would have usually had, a hot dog, chips, soft drink, and lots of chocolate from a show bag (or two). This year I decided to take my bottle of water and that was it, I managed fine, and I did not have less fun because I didn't have a sausage on a stick. In fact I had more fun because I knew I didn't need it. Plus I walked around for over three hours, so I am sure those chips won't touch my hips!

Today I have started a new rule:

"No exercise on Sunday night", I need to have at least one night that I know I can just sit back and become one with the sofa, and of course Australian Idol night is the one. Next week I will try to make sure I exercise during the day instead.

I am very proud of myself because today I ate an apple when I had a sweet craving, why didn't anyone tell me apples are sweet? This changes everything.

A group of my girlfriends, who are bound together by

our past embarrassing nightclub antics and teenage-hood drunken songs, get together every now and then. We used to party pretty hard together every weekend; that was when good friends brought tequila!!! But only see each other now once every few months for lunch or a night out. Of course they are all still skinny, childless, and have expensive clothes. I am not bothered by that though, what bothers me is that every time I see them, at least one of them has to say "Anita you look like you have lost weight". This comment is not a compliment, I have not lost weight; in fact I have stayed the same size for the past three years (not including pregnancies of course).

These comments clearly tell me that I am the "DUFF" Designated… Ugly… Fat… Friend… of the group; and that they need to make me feel good by saying I look lighter. Instead it makes me feel even fatter and even more isolated. The next time I see them they are going to mean it!!! And hopefully I will not be so isolated from the group and be able to wear more stylish clothes… I CAN'T WAIT!

DAY FORTY SIX

Today I met a guy who has lost over twenty kilos in the past three months, he looks great. Pity he hasn't bought any new clothes yet, but he says he feels like a new man regardless. He told me he had done it on a no carbs diet, he went through some of the rules for me, and basically he is living off red meat and whiskey?

I can't see how this could be good for you…I also can't see how he will maintain his weight when he stops this diet. I think my plan is much more realistic, so far I have lost a little over five kilos and I have only slightly changed my eating habits. I would also recommend that if you do want to lose weight you should consult a doctor, I know they always say that, but it is cheaper than going to a weight loss clinic! What many people don't realise about drastic diets is that they can do nasty things to your body, why do you think all the celebrities have so much trouble getting pregnant?

Anyway, today I weigh 89.4kgs and I am starting to feel better about myself. I still have 4.6kgs to go before I can go to my concert, which is twenty-two days away. This is achievable! I am going to do it!!! I have also been invited to a fancy dress Halloween party the following week, I would love to be able to rent an exciting costume, usually I wouldn't even walk into the shop, in fear of laughter.

By the way, the kids and me had take-away for tea tonight, I only had a regular chocolate thick shake and some of the kids chips and nuggets though. This was far less than my usual and far cheaper!! I then did 30 minutes exercise.

DAY FORTY-NINE

I am only three kilos away from my pre-Logan weight now! I weigh 88.8kgs and am feeling great. Although I must admit yesterday was terrible, I spent the whole day thinking about food and even stole some chocolate bullets from my Mum's house. I suppose dieting is just like being an alcoholic, there are good days and bad days. I am lucky I am not an alcoholic because I would be off my head right now.

In the past I have been quite obsessive about food, on the bad days I have been, somewhat psychotic. For example I have (and am ashamed to admit it) done sexual favours for my husband in order for him to go to the shops and get me treats. I have even been so desperate that I once had sex with him for a snack size chocolate bar! What a psycho!!! I am lucky we are not rich, otherwise I would probably be much fatter, and my husband would be smiling from ear to ear!

I am sure you are convinced of my food obsession now…But just remember I do not recommend bargaining sex for food…if you can't be bothered going to the shops then you are already too fat…you can do without it…Stop Eating!!!

I now have two and a half weeks to lose four kilos, I

know this is a little unrealistic so I am not going to go crazy. Instead I will up the exercise and be more diligent with my food intake. I will not eat hot chips for seven days (I hope). Today I tried on a top, which a few months ago I could not have worn in public, this morning it fitted. Ok it was a little tight and not quite flattering, but I am determined to look great in it at the concert. I can't wait!

DAY FIFTY

I can't believe I am at day fifty; I haven't lasted this long at a diet since I was seventeen, and even then I didn't make it much further. When I was in my final year of high school my, now ex-boyfriend and I became fast food freaks, every night he would come and pick me up and we would go and hang outside McDonalds with our mates. Of course it always involved a thick shake and fries regardless of whether we had already had tea at home.

I slowly got fatter, and one day my boyfriend's brother said I had the body of a MAN, another crushing blow!!! I joined Weight Watchers and lost quite a lot of weight, back to my pre "Maccas" weight yay, but as usual I didn't finish, I stopped going with 3kgs left. Don't ask me why, I am still questioning it myself, I suppose it was too easy, I thought I could sneak in more and more crap over time and it wouldn't make any difference. Well three months later I had already gained back half of it.

I slowly gained it all plus more until I was twenty when my boyfriend and I split up, we just weren't meant to be. This gave me motivation; I bought my first unit and moved out of home. I had very little money so I lived off crumpets and cordial. As I was a free woman again I decided to spend more time with my girlfriends. Of course this involved heavy drinking and very little eating. Eventually, it turned into heavy partying and almost no food. I lost around 15 kilos and around 1/3 of my brain cells. On my twenty-first birthday I weighed 75 kilos. It was then that I met my darling husband, a shy and sexy young man who did not have a weight problem (until he met me!).

We fell in love, purchased our first picket-fenced house and settled in with our German Shepherd all within the space of a year. We then became home-bodies (or large-bodies), we started to eat, as if we were storing food for the winter. Even though we had no responsibilities, no children to worry about we were even lazier than we are now. We ate a lot of take-away and had many late night trips to the deli, for ice creams.

Eventually we decided it would be fun to have a baby (boy were we kidding ourselves), I began the pregnancy at 86 kilos. I decided I could eat whatever I wanted to, because if I craved it then of course that meant the baby needed it. Some how I don't think Logan needed 20 litres of gelati icecream or a never ending supply of chocolate biscuits.

I weighed in at 110kgs on the day of Logan's birth, I was twenty-three. I ate so many servings of hot chips when I was pregnant, that my husband thought Logan might actually resemble one. After the birth I looked and felt like a swollen Michelin man. Sorry ladies, when you have your child you only lose around four kilos on that day (if you are lucky), my sister thought she was just going to fit into all her old clothes after she had her first baby, of course for everyone except Elle McPherson this is not the case. She then spent her whole time in hospital wearing her nightie. Isn't it great to be a woman!

Logan was not an easy baby so I had no motivation to exercise. One day after hours of him crying, I finally got him to sleep by driving around in the car, as my reward I went through McDonalds drive thru and had a grease feast, I enjoyed the peace and quite while I gained half a kilo. My very bad eating habits continued, I went on various diets and in eighteen months I had only managed to get down to 97 kilos.

As if the first baby was not sleep depriving enough, we decided to have another baby when Logan was one and a half. The morning sickness was not pleasant, OK it was bloody disgusting and I wanted to die. I lost weight in the first trimester, but don't worry I made up for it, eating what ever I wanted for the next six months (I obviously didn't learn anything the first time). I must admit I did feel quite cosy as a plump pregnant woman.

Well anyway I weighed in at 110kgs again at Alexander's birth, July 2003. But, this time I had a secret weight loss weapon…breast feeding (I was unable to with Logan). I lost twelve kilos in five months of not dieting, what a lovely feeling, Alex was literally sucking the fat from my body.

Of course nothing lasts forever and after five months, he got teeth, I had to choose "weight loss or nipple loss". So I accepted I was never going to be skinny and started him on formula. Disaster struck! I gained 3kgs in one week; the easy road was over baby! I then joined Weight Watchers for the fiftieth time!!!

So that is how I got to where I was fifty days ago. I have lost a total of twenty-two kilos in fourteen months. Not bad, but this time I am going to stick at it until I reach my goal. And if I decide, in the future, to try for a girl, perhaps I will realise, that you cannot get away with over eating during pregnancy! It is not worth it!

Me aged 14 &
Toni aged 12, 1993

Aged 15
Before my
Year 11 river
cruise, 1994

Aged 16 at
Year 12 ball

With my good friend Emma
'The Instigator', Feb 1999

Aged 22, eight months pregnant – Dec 2000

Aged 23. Minutes after Logan was born – Feb 2001

Aged 25, Ten minutes before my Caesarean – July 2003

Me, 23 and Jai, 25 yrs old Our
Wedding Day – Jan 2002

Photographer: Carol Darby

Me and Toni,
aged 20

My Inspiration
photo. Taken on
Logan's 3rd
Birthday
– Feb 2004

My sister Toni aged 23, my brother Ben aged 22, Me aged 26 – April 2004. Ben's engagement party.

Day 52

DAY FIFTY ONE

Today I ate 70gms of chocolate…argh…why? I had only intended on eating 38gms. I bought a double pack of Turkish Delight chocolate (which is less than 2g saturated fat per serve) and gave one to my sister. After lunch we ate them, and we were satisfied. This is where I went wrong…my son did not want his chocolate, so as it was already open I just started eating it…my god, when will I learn? I then ate a small chocolate frog after dinner. I felt gross so I made up for it by doing 7.9kms on the cross trainer.

I have done quite well today, again implementing a high fibre cereal instead of a sweet morning tea; this lasts nicely till lunchtime and is also good for your intestines, yay! I am not a cereal person when I wake up, give me vegemite toast any day. I weighed in at 88.2kgs this morning and have lost two centimetres off my waist in two weeks.

I am about to start work on a big assignment for uni, it is going to be hard for me to avoid eating whilst sitting at the computer for hours. Ever since I was in high school I have enjoyed chocolate whilst studying. Luckily, I am flat broke and can't even afford to buy a Freddo…tonight I should be safe.

DAY FIFTY THREE

Well today I weighed 88.4kg and I am about to spiral out of control. For some reason I have just stopped being careful with my food intake. I have not been eating proper dinners, and just snacking all evening. This is going to stop now! Especially since I just worked out my new BMI to be 30.5, my god I am still obese…arrrrgggghhhhh!

It is time to get serious. I know I keep saying this, but I am twelve days away from my concert and I somehow doubt that I will lose 3.6 kilos between now and then. It is time for a rethink. Ok, in the past I would have said "well stuff it then", if I am not going to achieve it I may as well just eat badly again. Not any more. I am readjusting my goal to two kilos in twelve days, I will not weasel out of this challenge by claiming a lack of time.

I will weigh 86.4 kilos in twelve days!!!

In accomplishing this I will achieve two goals:

1. To be back at my pre-pregnancy weight
2. I will be under 30 BMI, and no longer obese… yay!!!

DAY FIFTY FIVE

Last night I went out for dinner with the girls. My weight conscious buddy, Monique, picked me up. As soon as she saw me she told me I looked great. I believed her. She's one of only a few who say it genuinely. We were discussing many things on the way to the restaurant, most of which was gossip catch up. It's funny how our conversations always lead to weight loss. No we are not boring, it is just that we are the only two members of our group who have ever needed to watch what they eat.

Monique is skinnier than me, but she does have a BMI over 25. We were discussing how hard it is to lose weight and why we are so obsessed with food. We are so obsessed that we even talk about being obsessed. After I had spent ten minutes describing my diet, and my success so far, Monique asked what I had planned to eat for dinner. I could have said salad, I probably should have, but I didn't want to bind myself to that. Instead I suggested that on our girly dinners the diet does not exist. We both agreed that would be a great idea.

We shared a deep fried Camembert, garlic bread and wedges, I don't know if there was anything more fattening on the menu; we certainly did a good job of finding it. To top that off I drank three bottles of wine cooler and had two cigarettes (no, I don't normally smoke). Boy when I say no diet, I mean NO DIET!

Then just when I thought I was the most food-obsessed person on earth, Monique proved me wrong. We were comparing our new mobile phones and the photos that we had stored on them. Of course I showed everyone pictures of my kids and of my house. Monique showed me pictures of the food from the wedding she had recently attended, and the enormous dessert she had shared with a girlfriend recently…Oh my god…I am not the only one!!!

Luckily I was far too embarrassed (and poor) to get cake after dinner, so I really didn't do too badly. We spent the next half an hour, in the car on the way home, repeating our usual ritual of gossiping about the people that we just had dinner with. Especially the "low carb" couple, who made a point of leaving their potatoes on their plates and letting everyone know how much weight they had lost. Pity they will also lose their eyesight and limbs if they continue their fad for too long.

I had such a great night; I love catching up with friends. Unfortunately, I also love the food that is involved with the catching up. But I refuse to let weight loss rule my life though, and I plan to enjoy these nights out in the future. That is why you cannot deprive yourself. It must be realistic!!!

DAY FIFTY SEVEN

All I can say today is that moving more than 300 brick pavers from the front to the back of a house is good exercise!

My arms are too sore to write anything else, good night…

PS. I am still obese…

DAY SIXTY ONE

Well I have had a bit of a set back; it's called fish and chips. Last night, it was my husband's birthday, so we had take-away for tea. After I had finished gorging myself I felt gross. I was not feeling euphoric or happy. I really could have done without it.

Still feeling sick, I decided that maybe a piece of chocolate cake might make me feel better…no…what about a chocolate bar…no…when will I learn? You can't get high from food!!!

I have all these preconceptions that equate to me believing that unhealthy food will make me feel great. But lately when I have fatty food I just feel bloated and unaccomplished. I am learning (slowly) that it's not the food that makes your evening fun it's what you are doing and who you are with. So tomorrow night I have arranged Brad Pitt to join me for dinner, this should help me to avoid food altogether.

I have decided that since I am now at day sixty-one I should reflect on the most important parts of my journey so far:

1. It is important to learn about the nutritional value of foods and how to read labels properly

2. Drink 1 litre of water per day (I know everyone says it but it's true, it works, in fact you are supposed to drink more)

3. High fibre cereal makes a great morning tea

4. Apples taste nice

5. Exercise really does make you feel good (better than a Mars bar)

6. Hot chips are spawned from the devil

7. So is chocolate

8. I am not the only person who is obsessed with food

9. Do not go on a fad diet, it doesn't work

10. So far I have succeeded, so I am not going to quit when I start to go off track

11. Fairy bread is for children, so is ice cream cake!

I am not going to tell you how much I weigh because I have stopped looking, all I can say is that I am not going to my concert!

DAY SIXTY TWO

I can't believe it. I weigh 88.8kgs today – that can't be right? It is though; I have tried moving the scales to fifty different positions. I have been so good for the last two days, now I really wish I had never eaten all that crap the other night!

Last night I kept on making excuses why I shouldn't exercise. So rather than bore you with the whole saga I have made a list of my and my friends most regularly used excuses to avoid such horror:

1. If I exercise tonight I will have a sweaty head, then I will have to wash my hair. It is too late for it to dry, so I would have to go to bed with wet hair, I therefore cannot exercise because you get sick if you sleep with wet hair

2. I will start fresh on Monday then I'll have a full week of exercise (of course Monday never comes!). This has got to be the most popular, when are we going to learn…

3. I vacuumed and swept the floor today so I don't need to exercise (this is reasonable but not in the long term)

4. I do plenty of walking at work, that's enough exercise (the idea is to increase your exercise)

5. I will wait until summer, and then I can go swimming (will you hibernate all winter?)

6. Then when summer comes the excuse is: The kids really hate going to crèche, it would be unfair on them

Despite all the excuses I did manage to succeed in the face of adversity, I completed 40 minutes on the cross trainer, yay! I really need to get my moneys worth from it this week as it is due to go back soon, oh damn. What a great excuse, unfortunately I am too poor to hire it again so I am going to have to think of a new way of exercising.

DAY SIXTY THREE

I am beginning to get bored of writing about myself so here is a list of my favourite tips to remember when you are on a diet:

1. Don't expect your husband/ partner to notice your weight loss straight away. Remember, they can't even find items that are staring them in the face, they are blind, don't take it to heart!

2. Don't play mind games with him either, you will only get hurt, they are simple creatures, they do not have ulterior motives. If he says, "you look fine" then you look fine.

3. Don't buy clothes that don't fit you, as an incentive. It doesn't work. I have various pairs of trousers in my cupboard which are no longer fashionable. My expensive 'surfy' cord trousers have a waist so high, that even if they did fit me I would be the queen of camel toe. Just give yourself other incentives instead, like days out, hairstyles or facials. These are a lot more satisfying!

4. Do not buy share packs of chocolate bars, it doesn't help, you will eat more than one at a time, come on you know you will. And by the way two snack size bars equate to one normal sized chocolate bar, I found this out the hard way. I was sure it was around five to one.

5. Don't buy something because it says 95% fat free, this is a scam. Look at how much the product weighs, for example, a large choc milk is 600mls if they advertise it to be 95% fat free that means it must be 5% fat, 600 x 5% equals approx 30 grams of fat. This is massive, so watch out!

6. Now I am still grasping this one myself. If you feel like a treat have one, a small one. Do not go round the house eating everything in sight as an attempt to avoid the Mars bar in the fridge. The truth is you will eventually eat the chocolate anyway so this way you avoid all the stuff in between.

7. Don't spend hundreds of dollars on weight loss branded foods. There are plenty of less expensive options just read your labels.

8. The last, but not the least, don't tell everyone at work that you are dieting; you do not need the stress. You especially don't need everyone in your office looking at your weight loss each day, or watching whether or not you are sticking to it. Plus, if no one knows, you will be pleasantly surprised when someone does notice the weight loss, that way you can feel confident that it is genuine.

DAY SIXTY SIX

Well I am very disappointed in myself. I have been in denial this weekend. I did not go to the concert, so I stayed home and ate crap instead. I feel as though I could just give up now. I keep thinking; that I don't mind being fat, I should just accept it and get on with life. Then I see my reflection in a shop window, or car door and realise I am kidding myself, I am repulsive, and I need to keep going.

I have decided to start all over again. Basically my goal weight is still 69kgs, so I have a little under 20kgs to lose in 15 weeks. I have revitalised my enthusiasm and am going to start fresh. I have said many times that I believe exercise to be the key to my diet, however I have also made many excuses not to do it. I realise now that there can be no excuses! Exercise needs to become a regular part of my life. I will not go to bed each day unless I have done at least 20 minutes of exercise.

Wish me luck; the weddings are only 14 weeks away. Oh yeah, I forgot to mention, both my sister-in-law, and my brother are getting married in January, on the same weekend. I am determined to look fabulous at both weddings; as I will be seeing many relatives whom I have not seen for years. I have always thought that Jai and I were considered to be the "fat couple", well not this time folks!!!

DAY SIXTY SEVEN

I have two things to discuss tonight.

Firstly I have discovered the secret to losing two kilos in one day…Breast Reduction. My friend Natalie, recently went from a size E to a C cup and she looks fabulous. The decrease in her chest size has really changed her figure, she looks like she has lost ten kilos, but she actually lost two kilos of breast tissue.

Me on the other hand am in desperate need of a breast enlargement. On the weekend I went out with my sister. I had no nice clothes to wear, so I borrowed one of her tops. What a laugh. My sister nearly wet her pants. It was one of those tops with the elastic boob tube bit that flares out at the waist, so you can't wear a bra. I looked like a twelve-year-old girl. You know how they have swollen nipples, before they actually develop real breasts. I am so embarrassed. You should have seen me before I breast-fed. I was a comfortable C cup but now my breasts consist only of large nipples and stretch marks.

Anyway, Jai said he would pay for an enlargement if I lose 20kgs. So I had better just concentrate on that. I have decided, as erratic as I am, to try something new. I have realised that changing my diet and introducing exercise into my life are two huge changes. Perhaps if

I try to do one at a time I will have more success. Here is my plan:

- For 3 weeks I will do aerobics every morning for half an hour
- I will continue to drink at least one litre of water per day
- But, I will not change my diet (I will not go silly either)

This will give me an idea of the effect exercise has on me, so that if it does nothing, I will have the best excuse of all.

DAY SIXTY NINE

Well I haven't quite started the exercise yet, but on the scales this morning I weighed 88.0kgs, which is great considering all my stuff ups lately. I had half a ham foot long from Subway for lunch and will have the other half for tea. So far today I have done very well!

Yesterday, my sister and I went looking for Halloween costumes. The lady at the local dress-up shop was one of those tactless people. She greeted us by saying "so you want costumes for the BIG girls", then went on to tell my sister "if you can wear a singlet out [to the shops], then you can certainly wear this", my sister was trying on blonde wigs which she wasn't used to, and was worried about how they looked. What a lovely lady! Toni decided that she didn't need our business and we left.

The party is on Saturday, three days away, I am hoping to look wonderful, I am dressing up as Uma Thurman from Pulp Fiction. Maybe I can rename it "Plump Fiction". I am sure no one will know who I am, but I don't care, I just love the black wig.

DAY SEVENTY ONE

Ok, the Uma Thurman thing is just a recipe for disaster. I will only feel self-conscious, so I have decided to just go as a person in a black wig.

I have now lost a total of seven kilos. I know it has taken me 10 weeks to do it, but my doctor said that half a kilo a week is what I should aim for. It does make sense that; the longer it takes you to lose the weight the more likely it is that you will have changed your lifestyle for good.

The other night I was watching a makeover program and I saw liposuction being performed. Oh my god! I am now having second thoughts about that tummy tuck. It was so gross, and the colour of the fat was like cooking oil, all yellow and clumpy. I really wish that when you ordered a large fries from McDonalds that it actually looked like the fat that they were sucking out, I know I would not want to eat it then.

I also think they should put warnings on food just like on cigarettes: "Eating excessive amounts of deep fried food can lead to obesity, heart disease and low self esteem". At least then I would have it staring me in the face. My sister thinks they should put a mirror panel on all chip packets, so you get to see yourself getting fatter. I think it would work better than the smoking warnings - I don't know a single person who takes any notice of them.

I am going to the party tonight, wish me luck, hopefully I can just relax, have a good time and not stress out about how I look. I know…a bottle of champers should do the trick!

DAY SEVENTY TWO

The party was great. I ended up dressing up as the Fairy Godmother from Shrek 2 – my sister was Princess Fiona, and she did a damn good job of it too. We really went all out with this one, and we were all hyped up until we got there. We pulled up at my friend's house at the same time as two other cars, so we decided to wait and see their costumes before we got out of the car. Oh my god…they did not have costumes on! We were cracking up, how typical, the one night we can actually go out together and we were about to be humiliated.

After fifteen minutes in the car, we decided to brave it and just go in. Once we got in the house there were other people dressed up, and even one guy had his face painted, yay! We had a great night; I got very drunk very quickly and feel fine today. Of course that is partly due to my pancake and milkshake "morning after breakfast regime".

During our childhood my sister and I were both quite thin. Then when high school hit, my sister, who wasn't interested in sport at all, gained a small amount of weight. It was more puppy fat than anything. I still feel guilty that I used to pick on her and call her "fat", but what are big sisters' for right, and she was never an angel. Anyway, she wasn't fat; in fact I would love to be the size that she was when I called her that. She was probably less than my goal weight of 69kgs.

Whilst she was in year twelve she met her Husband, Tom, they fell deeply in love and were engaged within months. A few months later she was pregnant (all she ever wanted was to be a mother). She, like me, gained a lot of weight during her pregnancy; she started at 70kgs and gave birth to a boy in March 1999, she weighed 92kgs, a gain of 22kgs. She was shocked at the small amount of weight lost straight after the birth and she really didn't lose any more until she got pregnant again nine months later, this time she actually lost weight during the pregnancy. I suppose this was due to the exercise involved with the toddler and also the lack of time to eat. She also credits her weight loss to her intense cravings for strawberries and lots of water intake over summer. After her daughter was born in August 2000, she weighed 86kgs.

Like me, she has been dieting on and off since then. But what really made me realise that I was extremely overweight, was when Logan was ten months old and I was being fitted for my wedding dress. My sister was also being measured up for her bridesmaid dress and all of her measurements were less than mine. I couldn't believe it, I had always considered myself to be the skinnier sister (I use that word loosely, see the wedding pictures). Since then I have always compared our weights and would love to catch up to her soon!!! She is about 7cms shorter than me so I don't have to be her weight exactly. The problem is that lately she is losing weight as fast as I am. She currently weighs 81kgs.

This just gives me even more motivation because I don't want to be the fat sister at our brother's wedding. Don't get me wrong, I don't want her to be either, I think it would be great if we both looked stunning!

DAY SEVENTY FOUR

It is only 12.41pm and I have already had Hungry Jacks fries and a chocolate shake. What is my problem???

I know what went wrong…I did not eat breakfast!!! I then drove to the airport to pick up Jai, and on the way back I was starving. They really need to invent drive-thru Subway. I couldn't resist, and it was easy, yummy and filled me up. This afternoon I am going to go for a walk because I feel disgusting. I only have a couple of months left and I seem to have forgotten I am trying to lose weight. Oh yeah, I haven't started that exercise thing yet either. You must be so disappointed in me, I am trying to motivate the people of Australia and yet I am still consumed by take-away.

My BMI is 30.38, I am so close to only being overweight, come on I can do it!!!

DAY SEVENTY SEVEN

I am so frustrated today. I am still 87.8kgs I have not lost a single gram! I am so in denial of what it takes to lose weight, but I am going with a friend to Fremantle today so I need to stay in denial for one more day. The tough stuff will start tomorrow!

DAY SEVENTY EIGHT

I have just gotten back from a picnic at the beach with Jai and the boys. I feel exhausted and accomplished at the same time. Of course I didn't swim, I couldn't do that to the innocent beach goers, but I walked and played with the kids for over an hour instead. This week has been all about increasing my activity level. I aimed to do some sort of physical activity each day and so far here is the exercise I have done this week:

Tuesday. Walked to park with kids and played on the playground (I couldn't even go across two bars on the monkey bars, what a girl's blouse). 40mins

Wednesday. Brisk walk with Alex in pram around Carramar. 30mins

Thursday. Walked to the Park. 20mins

Friday. Walking around Fremantle, I purposely parked about 10 minutes away from the restaurant and then went for a brisk walk around the markets and shops. 40mins

Saturday. Beach with boys, no naughty food in picnic either only vegemite roll and diet coke. 40mins

This may not seem like much, but usually I wouldn't

have done any of it. I have decided that it is time to get serious. I was at the shops this morning and I saw a friend whom I haven't seen for over three months, what a bummer, she has lost a lot of weight. Last time I saw her she was the same size as me, but since then she has had troubles with her gall bladder and cannot eat fatty food. What a good way to diet, eat well or die! This might sound easy but another friend of mine Amy told me that for her, losing weight is harder than quitting smoking, and god knows quitting smoking is not an easy feat.

DAY SEVENTY NINE

I took Alex for a walk today, and it was bloody hot. My new excuse for not walking is the flies – I hate them. The worst thing is I don't even know how many I ingested, I hope they are not fattening, what a waste!

I have worked out that in order to no longer be obese I need to weigh less than 86.7kgs. That sounds easy right? Wrong. I am a complete failure; I have still not lost any weight. What is worse is that I was reading an article about some skinny model who stated that she has never exercised in her life! What the hell? She says she owes her body to 'good genes'. That is so fu*king unfair.

I really feel like giving up today. I am so pathetic that I even decided to get pregnant just so I had an excuse to stop this diet…don't worry I have gone off that idea. One trip to the shops with the boys is enough evidence that two children are plenty.

DAY EIGHTY

Ok, when are men going to realise that begging for sex is not attractive. In fact it makes them seem like pathetic losers who can't even get a lay. My husband (after three years of marriage) has finally discovered that by not asking he may actually get a nice surprise, sex! My friends and I often discuss this issue and find it hard to believe that this was left out of our Year 10 sex education. They really should have warned us that at first sex is fun, then it's a chore, then it's a bore, then it's no more!

I am sure that men have similar frustrations, but until we can understand each other's predicament we're screwed. I have tried to imagine what it would be like to be horny 24/7, this is not easy, but I have imagined that having a giant clitoris hanging against my body would probably be cause for arousal. So I understand, does this mean I care? No!

When we went to a 'teach your child to sleep' hospital, my husband so kindly expressed his sexual frustrations to a counsellor, this was her reply "men have sex to relax, and women need to be relaxed to have sex". I will never forget that comment, because it summed up all our problems in one sentence. I have gotten a lot better lately and have been using sex as a relaxation tool. Although it is a lot like exercise, I have lots of excuses why I shouldn't do it. I especially like to use the "I can't be bothered getting out of bed afterwards to wash myself, let alone getting undressed in the first place" excuse.

One trick I have learnt is not to put it off. You will eventually have to do it and then you may end up feeling like a prostitute. It is much better to do it during the day, you can surprise him, and you won't be too tired to initiate it. Even better, morning sex, you are going to change and shower anyway right? Just think a surprise sex is better than three "have to" sexes and he will be happy to hang out the washing afterwards!!!

Another trick I have learnt is to go to bed naked He will get a great surprise when he gets into bed, and you don't have to get changed. I have found that this also helps me to get in the mood, as the sheets feel nice against my skin, and for a split second I imagine myself at a five star resort. Then the big hairy husband gets in the bed and reality kicks in. Oh well give it a shot you won't regret it!

You may be wondering what this has to do with weight loss. For me it is very significant because only when I feel good about myself do I feel comfortable to have sex in the first place. Men on the other hand either don't care or think they are sexy beasts.

My husband tries to help by informing me that semen is good for weight loss…Great give me a super sized sperm sundae please, yummy. He also reminds me that sex is exercise and that it will help to increase my metabolism, therefore promoting weight loss. Thanks honey! Maybe he should write a book too!

DAY EIGHTY FOUR

I have done the unthinkable. I have phoned and enquired about a metabolism, blood test type weight loss centre. I know I said I wanted to go it alone, but it is too bloody hard!!! Why can't it be easy??? I am going to an information session on Monday; I will let you know how it goes.

This week has been pretty full on. I have had a job interview and three end-of-semester exams. Of course this additional pressure has led to bad eating habits. I have had take-away three times and just topped it off with Chinese and half a bottle of champers (I had to celebrate the end of my second year).

I cannot believe I am even writing this book. I am really not doing very well at all. I mean seven kilos in eighty-four days is pretty shocking. It would be so easy to quit right now. I have a loving husband and children who don't care about my size; I could go on living life as an obese woman quite comfortably.

But I wouldn't be happy, and that is what matters, I will not quit!

DAY EIGHTY FIVE

I am so bummed; it has just occurred to me that perhaps the reason why both of my future sisters in law don't want me in their weddings is because I am a fat pig. I would ruin the photos and would have to get a dress made especially for me. Of course they may have just decided not to include me because they don't particularly like me. Or perhaps it has nothing to do with me as a person…My god stop worrying…argh!!!

Of course now I am getting obsessed with my fatness even more. It's funny how a simple thing like not being picked in a wedding can make you start to question everything about yourself. My god I feel sorry for all those people who got picked last in sports, maybe we should include rejection as an excuse for over eating!!!

I know I am probably just paranoid and their decisions were not deliberate, but at the moment I feel as though everything reflects on my negative body image. I will try to be more positive!!! My husband's sister has asked me to do a reading instead, so I will embrace it and be grateful for the inclusion.

The one positive thing that has come out of my being rejected twice is that I am now more determined than ever to lose my weight and publish this book. I will be successful and prove to everyone, that when I say I am going to do something, I really will, and I will kick ass at it too!

DAY EIGHTY SIX

I have had a huge clean out of all my old paper work today; it is good exercise, that's for sure. Whilst rummaging through it I came across my old Weight Watchers record books, I thought I would share them with you:

The first one begins on 15 August 1995 (I was in year twelve) probably the week after the chin incident. I started at 71kgs, can you believe that, that is now almost my goal weight! I only went for six weeks but I lost 4.3kgs, I finished on 66.7kgs. I am so disgusted in myself right now.

The second one begins on 28 August 2001 (Logan was six months old). I weighed 98.6kgs, which is 32kgs heavier than in 1995!!! I went for sixteen weeks and only lost 3.5kgs.

The last one was from this year, I started on the 8th of February 2004, I went for eleven weeks. I started at 96.9kgs and I got down to 93.0kgs, a loss of 3.9kgs. You may wonder why I stopped going. The answer is simple. I wasn't losing weight quick enough so I quit! I now know that this is ridiculous, a loss is a loss and I have plenty of time to lose weight.

So as you can see Weight Watchers did work, you just have to be realistic. It's not meant to be easy. How many times have you planned a diet then when we reach our goal date we think, "shit I had all that time and I haven't even lost a kilo". What's worse is that even if I lost a kilo a year since high school I would be at around 60 kilos right now!!! Why are we so impatient??? Imagine if I could lose another five kilos per year until I am thirty…That would be the best birthday ever!!!

DAY EIGHTY NINE

I can't believe I am only half way through and I have still only lost seven kilos. Looks like a race to the finish now though, so I have bumped it up a notch. Today and yesterday I did forty-minute aerobics workouts. Afterwards I felt great, really rejuvenated. I have been eating well and have been totally focused on my goal. I aim to do aerobics six times a week. It's not so bad if you do it in the morning, then you don't dread it all day, and you can spend the rest of the day satisfied. Why would you eat crap after you have done a workout, right?

I didn't end up going to the metabolism weight loss place; I got them to send me the info instead. After reading it I realised that, I am writing this book about how to lose weight, without having to spend hundreds or thousands of dollars. It would be hypocritical of me to turn around and say it can't be done on your own, when I know that it can. It just takes a bit of guts, and determination, and your brother and his fiancé seeing you in your aerobics outfit to get you through it.

One thing that it has motivated me to do is start my own weight loss support group. Instead of paying hundreds of dollars to be told to avoid the foods, that you already know you shouldn't eat, the customers would pay me ten dollars a month to ring them twice a week and check up on them.

I would also send emails to everyone to make them feel guilty if they have been bad, and keep them informed of other people's success stories. I could include recipes, jokes, weight loss tips and general lifestyle information in a weekly e-newsletter. This would be much less expensive, and far less time-consuming for the busy women of today.

There I go again, another project.

DAY NINETY TWO

I have done well this week, I have continued to do my aerobics each day and have been careful not to eat badly. I cannot understand why I still weigh 87.8kgs, what a bloody pain in the butt!

I did get some good news today…I got the scholarship! (The job interview I went to a week or so ago). This provides me with financial support for next year, a guaranteed twelve hours work per week while I am studying, and a position in the post graduate programme in 2006. I am so excited! After I got off the phone I jumped around the kitchen for half an hour (great exercise). Now all I want to do is have a packet of chocolate biscuits to celebrate. No, don't worry I didn't, but I bloody well wish I could!

I found a gorgeous dress today. It is black with uneven gold hemming. You know what I mean it is like a fairy costume at the bottom, probably about 3/4 leg length, with shoestring straps. It would be a great wedding guest dress, but they only had it in size 10 and 16. Problem solved, I only need to lose five more kilos and I will fit into the 16. The diet is complete and I can get back on with my life.

God, I am a psychopath!

Every minute of every day revolves around my body image, and what food to eat next. When will I be spared of this burden? It is making my life hell. I would rather be one of those jolly fat women, who are perfectly comfortable with their size.

DAY NINETY THREE

Today one of my friends told me that my book reminds her of Bridget Jones' Diary. I saw the second movie today, and decided that there is very little comparison. Come on, where is my romance? He is currently underground shovelling dirt and showering with fellow horny, and homesick men. Plus I don't smoke and I certainly don't wear big granny knickers, well only on special occasions. Ok I admit it I am a bit like her, but isn't every woman. I would much rather be likened to Carrie Bradshaw!

I did enjoy the movie, but unfortunately I spent the first half obsessed with the fact that she (meaning Renee Zellwegger) is not actually fat in real life, and wondering why they wouldn't just use a truly "slightly overweight" person to play the role. During the second half I was fixated on all the food Renee would have had to eat in order to gain so much weight. And I would like to know what bloody diet she went on to lose it all???

By the end of the movie I had realised that I need to just sit back and relax. After all it was just a movie, and a pretty good one at that. I conclude that if my book ever gets made into a movie, I would prefer a fat person to play me, although on second thought, anyone who is good enough for Jack White is good enough for me!

DAY NINETY FOUR

I watched a documentary today called "Super Size Me"[7]. Oh my god! I am never eating McDonalds again (well I will try not to). The film is about a man who sets out to prove that fast food is bad for you. He goes on a "Mac Attack" for 30 days only eating McDonalds. I am embarrassed to admit that I could relate to this film in too many ways. And I would like to mention that the children of the United States of America have absolutely no chance of healthy lifestyles, unless the school lunches change drastically. I am grateful that in Western Australia the food served in the school canteens is much more nutritious.

So basically, the man's health was greatly affected by his binge. After only a few days he began to suffer physical and emotional symptoms of ill health and began to look exactly how I feel every day.

The one theme of the documentary that really hit home was the notion that fast food could become addictive and that various foods contain potentially addictive chemicals. As you have read I am a firm believer of this idea and decided to research this topic further. The following are segments of published articles, which may be of interest to you.

Scott McCann[8] has written an article, which like I did, relates anorexia and bulimia with over eating. This makes me feel better, because I was beginning to think that I had made it all up as a delusion and an even better excuse to keep eating. You know what I mean, I am an over eater, I can't help myself, really I MUST EAT!

The article is very well written, it is easy to read, and is not too scientific. He mentions many of the reasons why people over eat and states that:

"Most assuredly, overeating is a disease of addiction, just like drugs and alcohol, food addiction has all the progressive physiological and psychological maladies affecting the heath, social and economic qualities of life of the addicted."[8]

He also states that:

"Dr. Michael Rosenbaum, MD, Mill Valley California, believes that food in some people has a profound effect on the limbic portion of the brain. This portion of the brain is the control center of our emotions and memory; it controls several automatic functions such as body temperature, blood pressure, sleep, hunger, thirst, and even sexuality."[8]

Scott explains that just like narcotic drug addicts each over eater prefers a different food, he believes that these foods are often *"products such as bread, cakes, pies, crackers, and cereals such as Wheaties"*[8], he also mentions potatoes and rice as less common addictions. I would have to say I fall into the deep fried potato category.

Scott has a test for people, who think they might be over eaters. He states, *"Many members of Overeaters Anonymous have found that they have answered yes to many of these questions"*[8]. Here are some of the ones that I answered "yes" to, I got 17 out of 21 *"yes"*s:

1. *Do you eat when you're not hungry?*
2. *Do you go on eating binges for no apparent reason?*
3. *Do you have feelings of guilt and remorse after overeating?*
4. *Do you give too much time and thought to food?*
5. *Do you look forward with pleasure and anticipation to the time when you can eat alone?*
6. *Do you plan these secret binges ahead of time?*
7. *Have you tried to diet for a week (or longer), only to fall short of your goal?*
8. *Do you eat to escape from worries or trouble?*
9. *Do you feel lethargic or daze like?*

Scott believes that in order to treat this illness it is important to make a "plan of eating" which is *"the beginning of learning a new, healthier way of eating. It is a way of life, not a temporary solution. Unlike dieting, a plan of eating is not about deprivation. Choosing to follow a healthy plan of eating is a positive choice for life."*[8]

I truly recommend reading the whole article, and I do intend on finding out more about Overeaters Anonymous.

DAY NINETY FIVE

Wow, there is an Overeaters Anonymous office in W.A. I found them easily; just type "overeaters anonymous" and your state into your Internet search engine, if you don't have the Internet then just use the good old phone book. If you remember what it looks like! I will contact them soon…

Still on the topic of food addiction I found an article in the Better Nutrition Journal in Atlanta, titled Junk food Junkies. The article outlined the findings of Rockefeller University researchers. It is stated, *"that the consumption of fast foods can trigger chemical reactions within the brain making the consumer addicted to the foods."*[9], It also suggests that foods high in fat and sugar *"have the same results to the reactions caused by illegal drugs"*[9].

Another article, Is junk food addictive?[10] states that it is very *"plausible that humans can become addicted to high-sugar and fatty foods"*[10]. They go on to say that rats that withdrew from fatty and sugary foods showed signs of common drug withdrawal symptoms such as *"chattering teeth, anxiety and shaking"*[10]. The article concludes that the matter of addiction is continually debatable.

The one thing that all the experts have agreed on is that

an addiction to food should be treated like any other addiction. Now I just need to find out how the other addictions are treated...

DAY NINETY SIX

I can't believe it; I have been doing aerobics every day for over a week and eating fairly well and I have gained nearly a whole kilogram. I now weigh 88.6kgs. This is just a joke! I feel thinner and have heaps more energy, but I weigh more??? My sister reckons I am gaining muscle, god I hope so. I am really beginning to lose interest in this challenge.

I have found that since researching the food addiction stuff I am thinking about it more and more. I realised that I have always been addicted to something. When I was a teenager it was boys, of course. As I got older, I began to enjoy gambling, and I must say, it did pay off. I bought my first property with the $1500 I won on the roulette wheel. I had gotten to the point; at the age of twenty, that I would go to the casino on my own. I did have a problem. I am lucky that after I got married I was always too poor to go to the casino, or I would probably still be addicted. So maybe abstinence is the best treatment, but it's not so easy with a fast food outlet on every corner.

As curious as I am, I could not keep saying or writing the word "addiction" without properly understanding it's meaning. This morning I looked on the Internet here is what I have come up with:

Dr. Mezmer's World of Bad Psychology[11], describes addiction as:

"When the pleasure of anticipation outweighs the logical value of the object you are anticipating, thus making you pursue it even though further consumption of that object will get you sick, fat, broke, or otherwise brain dead. Thus, looking forward to one beer (or bag of chips, cigarette, spin on a roulette wheel, etc.) is not addiction, but looking forward to a tenth beer is; conquering Italy (particularly if you are Napoleon) is not an addiction, but conquering Russia is; playing a video game for an hour is not addiction, but continuously playing it for twelve hours is; and looking at one picture of Britney Spears is not an addiction, but relentlessly searching for all her pictures is."[11]

And for the more scientific of you:

"Addiction is defined as the compulsive need for and use of something that is psychologically or physically habit-forming, characterised by tolerance and by well-defined physiological symptoms upon withdrawal; Being abnormally tolerant to and dependent upon a habit forming substance. Addictions are of different kinds. They may be sexual addiction, gambling addiction, caffeine addiction, porn addiction, food addiction and etc."[12]

Amazingly they both mentioned food addiction! So why is it not mentioned in our society??? I suppose its better left alone; otherwise people might start having interventions for their fat friends. I do feel better now though, knowing that I am not the only one. I even found an article relating specifically to carbohydrate addiction.

So what's the next step??? I have admitted to the problem... I suppose I have to just go "cold turkey" like smokers and alcoholics. I will have to go through withdrawals too I suppose, perhaps I could go to a nutrition clinic to get detoxed??? One Powerball...

DAY NINETY SEVEN

Looking back on the last ninety seven days I can see that my best weight loss was when I was eating lots of Subway (and no hot chips or chocolate) and using the cross trainer regularly, so I will go back to that.

I had quite a nice experience today. My sister and I went looking for clothes to wear to the up and coming Tea Party concert. We tried all the fashionable little shops and found nothing, but in the "Hot Options" section at Target, I found a really nice dress. Of course I was not going to wear a dress (my legs are far too white and they haven't been shaved since 1999), but it was perfect to wear over jeans. I could not believe my eyes when I tried it on and it fitted…it fitted perfectly!!! No lumps or bumps either. Holy crap, it was a size 16!! Today had to be one of the best days this year!

I can't wait to see "The Tea Party", they are such an awesome band, especially live. The first time I saw them I was so motivated, I decided to write a book about myself, it only took me four years to actually do it. Now I have to finish it.

DAY NINETY NINE

I was talking to my mother-in-law about the Atkin's diet today. Her and her husband have been on and off it for over a year now, and they have had pretty good weight loss. I was explaining to her that there would be no chance in hell that I would be capable of doing the diet because I am addicted to carbohydrates.

We were discussing the health risks linked to the diet when she told me that Dr Atkins is actually dead. What??? Sorry but I am not going to do the diet of a dead man. Especially after I found that even though he did not die due to ill health: "In April 2002, Atkins was hospitalised after he went into cardiac arrest" [13] afterwards he stated that "it was no way related to his diet"[13]. For Christ sake, do people know this? Here is some other info about the diet that you might not know:

Atkins Diet – Claims[14]

- *You will lose weight fast*
- *You can eat large amounts of protein and still lose weight*
- *You eat very little sugar and white flour*

Atkins Diet – Drawbacks[14]

- *Initial weight loss may be quite fast, but is not always sustainable*
- *A ketosis-inducing diet may strain the kidneys.*
- *As many foods high in animal protein may also be high in saturated fat, your saturated fat intake may be too high for comfort.*
- *Giving up or severely restricting potatoes, corn, bread, fruits and vegetables and much more for as long as it takes to lose the weight, is not a user-friendly diet plan.*

This information was found at: http://www.diet-i.com/, I suggest that before commencing any fad diet that you check it out at this web site, there are hundreds of diets outlining the pros and cons. Also on the same web site the American Heart Association Media Advisory stated *"that people who want to lose weight and keep it off need to make lifestyle changes for the long term - this means regular exercise and a balanced diet"*[14].

I also found an article written by Dr Jeremy Sims it's titled Atkins – The Unhealthy Choice. Dr Sims outlines the health risks associated with the Atkin's diet. He states that[15]:

- *Long-term carbohydrate restriction can increase the risk of osteoporosis, with attendant risks of bone fractures, spinal collapse and nerve damage*
- *Those following the Atkins diet have a far greater risk of developing kidney stones – as much as double the risk*

He agrees that a balanced diet is the most sustainable in the long term, and that no diet should restrict fruit or vegetable intake.

God, I am starting to feel like I am writing my thesis, for that I am sorry, I will go now and stop being so analytical.

DAY ONE HUNDRED

I went to the Tea Party concert last night and I must say it was as good as I had expected. Thankfully, I felt confident in my outfit and found that many other overweight people also enjoy their music. This is a change from the skinny people I am used to seeing at nightclubs.

The one negative point to the night was my complete lack of control when eating. I was hungry on the way so I got my sister to go through a "drive thru" and get me a large chips, then when we got there my husband had something to eat so I asked him to get me some more chips (I know it sounds crazy but I was actually hungry). After the concert was finished there was a long wait to get out of the car park so my sister suggested we get something to eat. Again I managed to eat hot chips, FARK!!!

I am such a fat pig!!! I did not even feel bad that my husband's mate saw my disgusting binge; I am so ready for Overeaters Anonymous!

DAY ONE HUNDRED AND TWO

I am back on track. I walked for 45 minutes this morning and have decided to completely cut out all hot chips, chocolate and white bread. I was watching a show on TV last night and the lady said that the sugar in white bread could actually help you to produce more fat. I am not sure what this means but I will research it further at some point. In the meantime I do need more fibre anyway so I'm sure the change will be a positive one.

I can't believe I am at day one hundred and two. I feel as though I am completely losing control. I have exactly eighty days left. In reality I can only expect to lose a maximum of eight kilos in this time. This would give me a grand total of fifteen kilos and would still be a great achievement.

DAY ONE HUNDRED AND THREE

Today started off very well. I was good, with my whole meal bread, and raisin toast. I know probably too many carbs. I even had an apple today, which was nice. Disaster struck when my Mum rang me to see if I wanted to get take-away for tea. Why the bloody hell didn't I just say NO??? Instead I said "yes OK, what time, let's go soon cos I am starving". I am a complete lunatic.

To top it all off, the lady from Overeaters Anonymous phoned while I was half way through my dessert. She was very helpful and made me feel very comfortable. I only had to give her a few examples of my obsessive behaviour for her to say that I would be a suitable candidate for their program. She explained to me that obsessive compulsive eating is like a disease and the sufferer usually diagnoses it. She went on to explain that recovery is a long but very rewarding process. I felt great after speaking to her; I may have found what I am looking for! Why lose the weight when you haven't fixed the problem…

Of course it doesn't help that I won two movie tickets on my bottle of soft drink. Those bloody marketing guru's they control the world!!!

DAY ONE HUNDRED AND SIX

YES!!! I am now 87.6kgs, yay!!!

I have been working really hard this week. Except for my take-away indiscretion I have stuck to the no hot chips, no white bread and no chocolate. I feel great! I even noticed that the seat belt is not strangling me as much any more. I bloody hate that, not only are you fat, you are reminded of it every time you get in the car. I can't wait until the belt sits between my boobs again. Hang on maybe it's because I have no boobs that it has shifted. Well either way this weight loss will be worth it.

I have heard a lot about Gastric Bypass surgery lately, it was featured in "Super Size Me" and has been mentioned recently in magazines. Here is what I could find out about it[16]:

- *It is for people who are considered morbidly obese (BMI>40kg/m^2)*
- *There is no removal of adipose (fat) tissue*
- *The surgery can result by a "restrictive procedure" or a "malabsorptive procedure"*
- *Restrictive procedures decrease the size of your stomach, thus decreasing your food intake, and hopefully achieving weight loss, if this is not successful a malabsorptive approach may be taken.*

- *Malabsorptive procedures involve "bypass of the small intestine, thus limiting the absorption of calories"*

- *The risks and complications increase with the malabsorptive approach*

- *Combination of the two above procedures are also carried out*

When I tried to find an Australian surgeon who does this surgery I found the Victorian Obesity Surgery Centre, they specialise in Laparoscopic Adjustable Gastric Banding. I suggest anyone who is interested in finding out more should check out their website which is http://www.vosc.com.au, and is very informative and also has a BMI calculator.

As these procedures are mainly for people with BMIs of 40 or more I am too thin! How nice… am not a likely candidate. Oh well, I am going to have to keep doing this on my own. It's either that or go on a binge lasting a few months and then opt for the surgery. No!!! I think I will stick with my plan.

DAY ONE HUNDRED AND SEVEN

I am 87.4kgs this morning; yes I am back in the game.

I am so determined to lose this weight; I have even been thinking about what I would do if I publish my story. This is giving me a lot of motivation. I want to help as many people as I can to change their lives. I want to have weight loss support groups, not diet clubs, just places where people can go for education, advice and support. I would really love it if we could make weight loss a more acceptable health issue. Imagine if you could go to a support centre and just look around the way you would an optometrist.

Why do people who over eat have to be seen as disgusting? Why do we view people with mental health problems as "strange and unapproachable"??? That's right if you think you are a compulsive over eater that means you have a mental health problem!!! So next time you pass judgment on a drug addict, or schizophrenic or someone who seems just plain "crazy" remember that you don't know the full story of their lives.

Did you know that :

• *Over two million people in Australia experience a mental illness each year and that one in five people in Australia 18 years or older meet a criteria for a mental disorder.*[17]

• *Expenditure on mental health services ($3.0 billion) accounted for 6.0% of all health expenditure in 2001-02*[18]

It also occurred to me, whilst my two boys were running around the kitchen bench (for almost an hour), that if I did manage to publish my story I might even make a few dollars out of it. Thus, I would be able to afford to buy a block of land in the country. God knows I need to take the kids into the big outdoors. They really do need a couple of acres!!!

DAY ONE HUNDRED AND EIGHT

I am 87.0kgs this morning, and with just under eleven weeks left, I could still lose another eleven kilos.

I took the kids to a park today; we went for a bush walk, then fed the ducks, ate lunch and then played. Usually this would have killed me. Not today though, I felt great and even had plenty of energy to help the kids on the slide and other play equipment. I can really feel a change happening.

The best part of today was when I tried on my 'going out pants'. These are the pants I used to wear out clubbing when I was twenty-one, I have saved them all these years as a guide to my fatness. Well guess what? They fit! I could do them up easily. Of course there was a slight bulge above the waist but they were comfortable and felt great. My god soon they will be too big for me….how exciting!!!

DAY ONE HUNDRED AND NINE

I just realised that perhaps the reason why I have been having trouble getting to sleep lately, is because I am not actually tired! Wow, I have been going to bed at the same time as usual and finding that I am not able to fall asleep. Of course, it makes sense, I do feel more energetic and awake in the evening lately. It would be a bonus if I have given myself an extra hour per day. That would be great!

It could also be because I used to spend around two or three hours per night grazing on carbohydrates from the kitchen. I always went to bed full, so I was tired because my body was digesting all that food!

I took Logan to the pool today; Toni and I swam laps before we took the kids in. We forgot to bring our goggles so we only managed 400m but that's better than nothing. I would like to mention that the smell of hot chips and vinegar should be banned from all swimming pool areas. It's not fair; you do the exercise and then ruin it with chips. Toni sees it as cancelling each other out. That's fair enough but it means I didn't exercise today.

I am still wide-awake (at 8.45pm), so I am going to do a half hour of aerobics before my shower.

DAY ONE HUNDRED AND ELEVEN

Oh my god! I am no longer obese!!! I weighed 86.6kg this morning; this gives me a BMI of 29.96. I am stoked. It must have been all the exercise lately. Maybe I can get away with having my chips every now and then (what is my problem?). I just have to be very careful that the now and then doesn't turn into today and tomorrow!!!

I did twenty minutes of aerobics this morning and will do some more tonight. It seems that the more weight I lose the more motivated I am to keep going. I do have to be careful of sabotage though. I have come up with a theory – the theory of 'weight loss sabotage'. I believe that in 99.99999% of cases people stop dieting (before they have reached their goal weight) because of either one of the reasons below:

- **Overconfidence –** Your excess weight is coming off nicely, so you get confident, and begin to add bits and pieces here and there. You end up doing the Atkins Diet for breakfast and then the 'eat what you want' diet for lunch and then the no fat diet for dinner. Eventually you are on the 'I am pretending to be on a diet' diet.

- **Obligatory** – You give up due to an obligatory binge. Often this would start with a function or event, where you were "forced" to eat badly, or a friend giving you a box of chocolates. Following this you spiral out of control and then blame the event, or the person…

- **Impatience** – The weight is not coming off quickly enough so you, "unknowingly?" increase your food intake, almost ensuring that you will continue to not lose weight. You eventually stop dieting because you must be destined to be fat.

Of course, I have sabotaged myself in each of those ways, and even in this book I have used my Mum bringing me food as an excuse for sabotage. The fact is, that you can eat junk food, just not every day, or maybe even every week, especially if you are prone to binging and then going off track.

At this point I am not interested in having take-away at all because I would see it as a huge waste of all my hard work. However, if I was invited to dinner I would not say "no" just because I am dieting. You just need to be aware that if you have a "naughty" night you need to work harder for the rest of the week, and remember you don't have to have the most fattening thing on the menu. Even McDonalds have healthy choices these days. Ok they may not be as nice but neither is an extra half a kilo on your arse!!

Speaking of dinners I have one at a buffet on Thursday night, wish me luck.

DAY ONE HUNDRED AND FOURTEEN

What is the world coming to? Today when I answered the phone there was a recorded message which said "Hello, we have an important message for you, please hold", what the hell??? I proceeded to hold on the off chance that it was someone calling me about my million-dollar cheque. After about three minutes I began to realise that almost all of my bills are overdue and it would probably be some money hungry company requesting a payment. I hung up. There is no way that I am going to have people ring me to put me on hold! What a joke!!!

An hour later I got a text message from my sister whom had just received a text message from her video shop, the message stated that her videos were overdue. Oh my god!!!

And, you know what, I am having trouble getting my head around the power shortages we are being threatened by this summer. They suggest we decrease our use of air-conditioners and pool pumps. What I don't understand is that the same power company actually gives away prizes to the house with the most impressive Christmas light display? Surely this is a much greater waste of power!

Anyway, on the topic of weight loss, I weighed 86.6kg

again this morning. I am not worried though because it has been very hot lately and I have been drinking lots of water. Also at dinner last night I ate lots of rice and had two too many bread rolls. But you have got to be proud of me, I did not even taste the dessert, even though there was an abundance of desserts to choose from, from ice cream to pavlova to mud cake. I just wasn't interested, especially at 9pm at night, when I know it would just sit in my stomach and turn into fat cells while I am sleeping. I am proud!

DAY ONE HUNDRED AND FIFTEEN

I am seriously considering throwing out my scales, because this morning I weighed 86.8kgs. I know this can't be right I have been so good. I felt like such a loser, definitely the most vulnerable "binge" time for me. I am lucky the day got a lot better…

Today I found the dress of my dreams; it is lovely and only $60. They only had size 10 and 14 so I asked the shop assistant if they could get a larger size. I couldn't believe my ears when she told me that the fourteen should fit me…oh my god, only a year ago I was not even able to buy clothes from that shop at all. I tried on the size fourteen and it looked fabulous, what is going on? I am losing dress sizes, but not many kilos??? Who cares, as long as I keep going, right?

I don't think I can throw those scales out just yet though; they are my security blanket at the moment. I feel as though I will just lose control without them, and then when I get on scales again in a year's time I will weigh 100kgs.

DAY ONE HUNDRED AND EIGHTEEN

I have not been so good in the past few days. Yesterday I had pancakes, hot chips and a milkshake all in one sitting, and then my husband and I went to the movies and had chocolates and popcorn. One thing I did accomplish was stopping when I was full. I would have had trouble with this in the past, and just finished the food for the sake of it. And I brought home some chocolates I never do that. I usually eat them all during the movie, then feel sick and tired all evening. Things have changed!!!

I do feel as if I am changing my attitude towards food. I am more accountable for the food I eat now, rather than actually believing that a packet of chocolate biscuits won't hurt me. I recognise now that they will harm me more than help me.

I have been good since then and been able to avoid a self inflicted sabotage!

DAY ONE HUNDRED AND TWENTY ONE

Holy crap, why am I doing this to myself, I keep saying that it is easy, but it is not! It is bloody hard!!!

Today I decided that I need professional help, so I picked up my info from Overeaters Anonymous and started to read it. I was very shocked to read the word God on the first page and even more shocked to learn that in order to beat my problem I need to firstly devote myself to a higher power.

For some this would be lovely, for me, it is not the best way to look at the problem. I admit I cannot judge a program that I have not tried, but in this case I don't feel comfortable trying. This discomfort stems from my "so called" religious, yet stripper watching, lying and drug taking ex-boyfriend who explained to me, in a lovely fashion, that because I was not in his religion I would ultimately go to HELL.

Since then I have preferred to keep my beliefs to myself and wished that every one else would as well. Basically O.A., relate their twelve steps to the Alcoholics Anonymous program. So basically sufferers go from step to step, finding themselves and healing their inner self along the way. I am going to have to take their word for it…

Perhaps I am too far-gone to even consider God as a weight loss option. I really do feel that this has to be on my terms. I know that I would not commit to the program fully if I am not fully respectful of its theories. So what now???

Once again I found no solace in Australian web sites, so I tried a worldwide search for help. I found out that, in America they consider Binge-Eating as an actual disorder. The web site of the National Institute of Mental Health in the United States of America made the following interesting points[19]:

- *Between 2 percent and 5 percent of Americans experience binge-eating disorder in a 6-month period.*

- *Symptoms of binge-eating disorder include recurrent episodes of binge eating, characterised by eating an excessive amount of food within a discrete period of time and by a sense of lack of control over eating during the episode.*

- *The binge eating occurs, on average, at least two days a week for 6 months*

- *The binge eating is not associated with the regular use of inappropriate compensatory behaviours (e.g., purging, fasting, excessive exercise) many with the disorder are overweight for their age and height.*

So they basically outline the disorder in the same way as Overeaters Anonymous and Scott McCann. The difference is that they take a more medical approach to the treatment; of course this is more suitable for me, as I am studying to become a nurse and have always been comfortable with science. The United States web site suggests that treatment for eating disorders should involve[19]:

• *Early intervention*

• *A comprehensive treatment plan involving medical care and monitoring, psychosocial interventions, nutritional counselling and, when appropriate, medication management.*

• *Establishment of a pattern of regular, non-binge meals, improvement of attitudes related to the eating disorder, encouragement of healthy but not excessive exercise, and resolution of co-occurring conditions such as mood or anxiety disorders are among the specific aims of these strategies.*

They state that:

"Research on interrupting the binge-eating cycle has shown that once a structured pattern of eating is established, the person experiences less hunger, less deprivation, and a reduction in negative feelings about food and eating. The two factors that increase the likelihood of bingeing-hunger and negative feelings-are reduced, which decreases the frequency of binges" [19]

I can admit that this has happened to me, I have decreased the amount of binges I am having and I have experienced positive results. The only thing now is to work on the actual habitual behaviour of the disorder.

Why am I still purchasing food with the intention of eating it in a binge like fashion? The binge itself is no longer satisfying, so why am I still doing it???

DAY ONE HUNDRED AND TWENTY THREE

Oh My God...

I have worked it out, I am not addicted to food I am addicted to shopping!!!

Of course, I enjoy buying the food, so consequently, one would assume I would also enjoy eating it??? So now that I no longer enjoy eating the food, I need to work on controlling the purchasing of the food. Next thing you know I will be starting up a grocery shopping support group.

I developed this new way of shopping a few months ago because we had no money, it doesn't cost anything and you still get your retail fix. The power of hindsight is very cost effective. I think I will use this technique a lot from now on!

Pretend Shopping – Anita Style

So here's what you need:

A pair of scissors
An exercise book
A glue stick
All the junk mail

Once you have gathered up your equipment, find a nice quiet place and get shopping.

Step One:

Cut out every item from every catalogue that you have the urge to buy.

Step Two:

Make a page in the exercise book for each shop and title it, I like to cut out the shops name from the front of the brochure (my husband finds this extremely obsessive, don't listen to others though, remember you are going to save money!!!)

Step Three:

Glue the items into the book, remember to include the price and the date, so you can compare at a later date.

Step Four:

Repeat steps one to three every week

Step Five:

After one month look back at your pretend purchases and work out which ones you still want.

Step Six:

Go and buy the items that you still want!

Step Seven:

Think of all the money you saved on those items you no longer want!!!

I am up to step six now and I can't wait; so far I figure I have saved hundreds of dollars. The best part is that it is so close to Christmas that I have the will power to wait for the after Christmas sales. I have even managed to wait long enough to get a newer model digital camera for the same price I would have paid two months ago.

Go for it people, it's time to shop!

DAY ONE HUNDRED AND TWENTY EIGHT

Christmas Eve

The last week has been bloody chaotic, the shops are like hell, and our refinance only went though yesterday. Thus giving me two days of shopping before Christmas. I have not been on the scales for over a week and to tell you the truth I really don't want to look.

I have been eating badly and have almost completely given up exercise. I am a big fat loser!

The most positive part of this week was, with my newfound wealth, my radical hair change. Yesterday I went to the hairdresser (the first time in six months). My husband's cousin is a hairdresser so I spoiled myself and visited her up-market salon. In the past I had asked her to make me a brunette (I am, and always have been blonde), but she was very reluctant saying 'It would be very hard to maintain' and that it probably wouldn't suit my fair complexion. Anyway this time I put my foot down, so she gave me lovely rich chocolate brown with a few caramel foils around my face. Oh my god!!! I look stunning! I love it sooooooooooooo much. I feel as though I have been completely rejuvenated.

I am a new woman!!!

So now that I have nice hair I need a nice body, I am totally back on track!!!

Oh god tomorrow is Christmas day, I just have to stay away from lollies, chocolate and bread, and I will be fine.

What a joke!

I forgot to mention that I received a Christmas card from Jai today, what a sweetheart, he even knew our address and bought a stamp all by himself. I am so proud of him, he is turning into such a gentleman!!!

DAY ONE HUNDRED AND TWENTY NINE

Christmas Day

Wow, I cannot believe how many people told me how great I looked today. My father-in-law who I have seen regularly in the past week finally realised I had lost weight and even told me I am looking attractive now.

Anyway, that aside, it must be the hair, because I had so many compliments I was beginning to think I should try out for the *Face that Stops a Nation* competition. My husband was so shocked when he got off the plane (he came home just for Christmas day), he nearly didn't recognise me. Of course all men think about is sex so his first comment was one along the lines of him never having had sex with a brunette before. What a lovely compliment?

In general the day was great, there was not a chocolate in sight, however I did eat a bacon croissant for breakfast and a ham and salad roll for lunch. I had a small piece of chocolate cake and some nibbles in the evening, but overall I think I did quite well.

I also did well in the present department, a few cds, dvds, a nice top, some cash and a recipe book among other items from my Mum, who also proclaimed that "Your hair looks good but I do prefer it blonde", I can't expect much more than that from her so I said "Thanks".

DAY ONE HUNDRED AND THIRTY

Boxing Day

I am still too scared to look at the scales; I really can't be bothered with this whole weight loss thing anymore. It is too bloody hot!!!

Unfortunately it is the heat that also reminds me of how fat and lazy I am. For some reason I really lose all energy when the weather gets above 35 degrees Celsius. My friends all love the summer and look forward to getting a tan and eating fruit. All I do is dread the fact that skirts are absolutely out of the question – that is if I don't want to lose the skin between my legs, or spend the next six months using nappy rash cream.

Yes… I hate summer!!!

The post Christmas sales started today, and on the TV there was an advert for a huge clothing sale. One of the brands they mentioned was called "Big Advantage" going from size 14 to 28. Firstly I would like to ask where the advantage lies if you fall into this size category? And secondly I wonder why the category is so bloody huge, size 14 people would be horrified to know that they are amongst the morbidly obese!!! They are making it so bloody hard to get into the 'No advantage' category these days, now we have to be a size twelve to even get a look in.

My life is getting harder by the day!

Oh yeah…Merry Christmas!!!!!!!!!!!!!!!!!

DAY ONE HUNDRED AND THIRTY TWO

Exactly one month until the weddings, I am in big trouble!

I got on the scales today, I can't believe it…I am obese again, what a disaster!!!

No I take that back, it is not a disaster. A disaster is the deaths of over 100,000 people from the tsunami in Indonesia, Sri Lanka and Africa. I can't believe that I am so worried about how I look when all of these people have been killed, injured or left homeless. That is a real disaster!

It makes you wonder if you should bother wasting your time trying to fit into the norm and making other people happy, when you could be dead tomorrow. I have thought about this a lot in the past few years, since the terrorism threat has become so real, but I can never come up with a good answer. I suppose all I can say is that I would love to have the opportunity to feel, even for one day, what it is like not to yearn for food or to feel so controlled by it's attraction. Once I have accomplished this diminished desire I will be ready for anything that the world can throw at me, if it lasts only for a week or for forty years I will be grateful.

So even though my suffering is in no way comparable to those who have lost loved ones, I hope that I can help others who may feel alone and suffocated by their complete lack of control. As for the tsunamis victims, all I can do is make a donation to one of the charities and pray (to whoever it is) that the world can come together to help these people. I truly believe that everything happens for a reason and that our lives are destined, I just have a lot of trouble understanding why thousands of children had to die for no apparent reason. I suppose I will never know why, that's what scares me…

DAY ONE HUNDRED
AND THIRTY FOUR

I am still very sad about the tsunami tragedy; the television networks are showing so much footage it is hard to avoid becoming obsessed with the disaster. I am so overwhelmed that I feel a complete lack of emotion today. The constant footage of body bags and mass graves is really getting to me. You try to distance yourself from it, almost as if it is not a reality, yet you can't stop seeing the images in your head.

I am having a hard time getting back on track…

DAY ONE HUNDRED AND THIRTY FIVE

New Years Eve

I had a sign today. The people who hired me the cross trainer phoned to see when I wanted them to drop off my new cross trainer. I hadn't really booked one, but I thought what the hell, so I bought a second hand one for two hundred dollars. They will deliver it next week.

I have decided it is time to get on with my life, I am not going to waste the next month, trying to convince myself that I could die tomorrow and all the hard work be wasted. I am not going to die!

I am going to be thin instead!!!

Happy New Year!

DAY ONE HUNDRED
AND THIRTY SEVEN

I can't believe it, I weighed 87.8kgs this morning. What a bastard! This is very bad news for me, basically it means that three take-away dinners and a small amount of chocolate (ok maybe a medium amount) in two weeks makes me gain 1.2kgs. This is a joke…

OK I now believe that I cannot get away with indulging in anything bad!

Sabotage again?

Luckily the cross trainer arrived today, I have drawn up a big poster saying:

'Lose 5 kilos in 28 days' I have attached our most recent family photo, the photographer must have thought I said "please make my arm look huge", because it seems to be the focus of the photo. Well it makes for good motivation.

I am going to make this work; the weddings are way too soon to be making excuses. I have bought both my dresses, one of which is a size 14. I am impressed, but I certainly need to lose the five kilos if I want to wear it.

DAY ONE HUNDRED AND THIRTY NINE

I have been doing well on the cross trainer and even increased the amount of time spent on it each day. I am averaging $1/2$ hr each night and feel great, why can't I be addicted to exercise?

Today I found a flaw in my "Subway is great" idea. I had no cash on me and needed to get something for dinner, I thought Subway would be a good choice. To my surprise they didn't take eftpos, what? I was then forced to try a chicken place (still aiming to get a low fat option) they also don't take eftpos. Ok now this is scary… the only place I could find that took eftpos was McDonalds???

Even though they do have the new taste menu, they are far too expensive for me, considering that a chicken roll with salad is around $6.00. At least Subway gives you a choice of size, and therefore price. And don't forget the stamps. I chose nothing, but I got the kids Happy Meals, I am disappointed in myself, even toast would have been better for them.

Why do I always use food as a reward? I do it with Jai as well, he is due back tomorrow, so I will try not to shower him in fatty burgers, pizzas and ice cream. He would much prefer to have me on a plate, sorry I know it's corny but it's true.

DAY ONE HUNDRED AND FORTY ONE

Yes! I am back on track big time.

I weighed 87.2kgs this morning, I have been eating well and drinking lots of water. I have been less obsessed with food, and to tell you the truth I can't even be bothered thinking about food anymore.

Since Jai has been home we have had Subway once and our special pancakes once, otherwise we have both been good. Jai is looking so good lately; he is such a sexy man!!! He is now down to 102kgs. Much sexier than the man he was a year ago, I can't believe the difference a year can make.

Today Jai and I were watching our friend Monique's wedding video (she got married in January 2004). When we saw ourselves we just burst out laughing! Jai called himself Fatty Daddy!!! He really did look quite huge. Luckily I was behind the camera for most of the night, but the glimpse of me doing the 'Bus Stop' was not pleasant.

In the past eighteen months Jai and I have lost a combined total of 35 kilos, another 35 kilos and we will be ready to have a 'skinny wedding' so we can replace the fat photos.

DAY ONE HUNDRED
AND FORTY THREE

I am 87.0kgs this morning, and very happy about it, there are twenty-one days until the weddings, I am at least going to get back below obese.

DAY ONE HUNDRED AND FORTY SIX

I am still 87.0kgs…

I am obsessed with food today, I keep thinking of having a binge. Instead I am going to write about it, here are my top seven addictive foods:

Foods I Should Never Start Eating

1. Peanuts or Cashews

2. M&Ms

3. Pringles

4. Corn Chips

5. Butter Popcorn

6. Chocolate Biscuits

7. Crackers

Ok, looking at that list makes me feel like a disgusting pig… mission accomplished!

DAY ONE HUNDRED AND FORTY SEVEN

I had some bad news today; the mother of one of my friends was diagnosed with breast cancer. The worst thing is that this year one of my mum's best friends lost her second breast, to breast cancer and is still having treatment. So far I have personally known four women who have battled with breast cancer. Something needs to be done to increase awareness. Did you know that[20]:

- *One in 11 women will be diagnosed with breast cancer before the age of 75.*
- *Breast cancer is the most common cause of cancer-related death in women in Australia.*
- *A total of 2594 women died from breast cancer in Australia in 2001*
- *Breast cancer is the second most common cancer among Australian women, after non-melanoma skin cancer.*
- *In Australia in 2001 a total of 11,791 women and 95 men were diagnosed with breast cancer.*
- *The risk of breast cancer increases with age. Almost 24 per cent of new breast cancer cases diagnosed in 2001 were in women aged 20-49; 49 per cent in women aged 50-69; and 27 per cent in women aged 70 and over.*

Holy crap! That is bloody scary, so I have decided to include the instructions for Breast Self Examination[21] (please go to this web site for full instructions and answers to frequently asked questions http://www.healthnetwork.com.au):

Breast self-examination: Looking after yourself

By Dr R McCoy

Regular breast self-examination does not take much time. Once a month is all that is required. Regularity is the key – it is better to spend a little time each month on examination, rather than spending a long time examining only occasionally.

The area of the breast includes all tissues from the collarbone to the bottom 'bra line', and from the middle of the chest to the armpit.

The breasts can be examined whilst lying or standing (such as while in the shower), however, the lying position is usually more effective for women with bigger breasts, as it flattens the breast tissue against the chest wall.

One method of self-examination is to imagine that each breast is divided into quarters, and the nipple and areola area is a fifth, central area. With the opposite hand, flatten the hand on the breast. Use the flattened fingers to thoroughly examine each of the five sections of the breast with a firm, small circular motion. With this technique, the grainy and clumpy tissues and structures within the breast should be detectable. A single lump is generally easily recognised as it feels like a pea or stone.

The website suggests that if you find a lump, you should get your doctor to check it out.

DAY ONE HUNDRED AND FORTY NINE

I am soooooo glad I got on the scales this morning guess what…I weighed 86.4kgs. That's the lowest so far, and the lowest in five years. So I spoiled myself, I bought three new tops and a pair of pants, all size sixteen, and I only paid $39 for the lot!!!

On the weekend I went out to lunch with the girls, I had a great time and caught up on all the goss. The best part was when I ordered a chicken ceasar salad. I am determined to decrease my potato intake, especially at lunch time. I am so proud of myself. We even went thirds in the bill. I really am growing up!

DAY ONE HUNDRED AND FIFTY ONE

I can't believe it….I have gone six days without deep fried food and have done half an hour of exercise each day!

Reality: If you exercise and eat well you will lose weight!!!

I weighed 86.0kgs this morning and am more motivated than ever. The weddings are less than two weeks away now and I am really looking forward to them!

DAY ONE HUNDRED AND FIFTY FOUR

The past few days have been very boring, I have been eating well and exercising each day. I have even achieved 35 minutes on the treadmill each day. I am so proud of myself.

I truly believe that a part of me has changed!

I feel liberated!!!

A kind of freedom from bad food…I have had no deep fried food for a week now, and the only chocolate I have had has been two Darrell Lea nougat bars.

Here comes the best part…I now weigh 85.2kgs!

I can't believe it, I am less than half a kilo away from a total loss of ten kilos in twenty-two weeks. And you know what…I don't care that it took me this long! I feel as though I have made a change in my life and will never go back to obesity again!!!

I weigh less now than I did when I got pregnant with Logan. I am so motivated, I just want to tell everyone!

I love the new me!!! I can't believe I have done this all on my own, no pills, or meetings, or fad diets, it was all me!

DAY ONE HUNDRED AND FIFTY SIX

I woke up today and weighed 85.0kgs, what an achievement!

But sadly I am a loser!!! I need to add another food to my 'should not start eating' list…chocolate Tiny Teddies. I ate half a box! What is wrong with me? I thought I was learning.

Doesn't matter, this is not going to stop me, I will do an extra 15 minutes exercise tonight!

DAY ONE HUNDRED AND FIFTY SEVEN

I did it, an extra fifteen minutes last night, wow the cross trainer is actually starting to be fun!

This morning I weighed a glorious 84.8kgs, bloody hell… I would love to say "it was so easy to lose ten kilos" but I can't. It was very difficult; in fact it was so hard that tonight I feel soooooooooooo exhausted, almost as if I need a break from the whole idea of weight loss.

To top it off, I am starving. I don't know why, but tonight I have eaten a McDonalds Chicken roll thingy, some chicken flavoured chip things, five low fat choc chip biscuits, and I do not plan on stopping yet.

The question is:

Is this a binge? Or am I truly hungry???

DAY ONE HUNDRED AND FIFTY EIGHT

Well last night did turn out to be a bit of a disaster. I ended up having two honey sandwiches and an icy pole on top of what I had already had. I just thank god that I did not have too much bad food in the house!!!

I got an email from one of my friends today; she has put an offer in on a house she likes. She attached the link to the house on her email so I could check it out. It is a lovely house and I'm very happy for her. One thing that struck me as ironic was the small table that was in the corner of the web page. The table outlined the amenities that were located near to her property. I could not believe that there are the same amount of fast food outlets as there are doctors, and that's not including the restaurants, check it out:

Hospital	2
Fast Food	24
Restaurant	22
Doctor	24
Bank	2
Police	3

I can't believe there are so many junk food places, we really are getting lazy aren't we?

Talking about lazy, I didn't use the cross trainer last night because I was too busy eating!!!

DAY ONE HUNDRED AND FIFTY NINE

Wow, what a weekend!

It was my sister in law's hen's night. We had a ball!!!

Her best friend planned the whole thing, stripper and all. I must say though the stripper was a bit of a let down…Why do they all have to be gay (or act gay)? I don't know why these men think that women are turned on by good choreography and hand stands. Seriously he spent more time looking at himself dancing in the window than he did being sexy…

It was fun to watch though, especially Jen's facial expressions when he had her rub baby cream on him. She certainly wasn't having any thoughts of regret for her upcoming nuptials. Maybe I have just uncovered the world's greatest conspiracy… Men have invented the 'gay stripper routine' so that nothing can possibly go wrong on the hen's night.

I had such a great night, I felt comfortable with everyone and didn't feel worried about what everyone was thinking about me. It was especially great that I got through the whole night without once considering food! Even one of Jai's very drunk friends who happened to be at the pub tried to hit on me…he reckons he didn't recognise me…

I did one hour on the cross trainer on Friday night and feel great today! Well as great as you can with hardly any sleep and a stomach full of vodka!!!

DAY ONE HUNDRED AND SIXTY ONE

This morning I weighed 84.6kgs, I am still very motivated I have been eating well and exercising every night. I picked Jai up this morning and this time we skipped our usual pancakes, maybe it will be every second trip home from the airport.

I am feeling very confident lately, I have been walking around the shops with my head held high, I am no longer worried about seeing old friends from high school. I know I still have a way to go but at least I am back to the size I was before I had kids!

My Dad loves to write poems and short stories and the other night he wrote this in support for all of us…enjoy!

TV promises[22]

There is no need for growing old,
I can retain my youth.
These wrinkles will all disappear,
the cream they offer will make it so.
The mighty Abswing will give me back
the body I had at twenty two and
Those little blue pills will give me back
the pride I felt at eighteen.

Peter Rondel

Me and Toni at the
Halloween party – Day 71

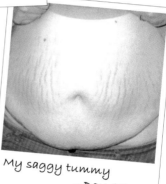

My saggy tummy
– Day 85

Family Photo
– Day 118,
Nov 2004

Pixie Photos, Joondalup

Before Jai's sister's wedding –
Day 164, Jan 2005

About four tequilas into
Jai's sister's wedding!

My birthday
night
– Day 170

My birthday gift from my wonderful husband

Me and Emma at Big Day Out, 2005 – Day 174

Me and Jai before my brother's wedding – Feb 2005

Anita

Jai

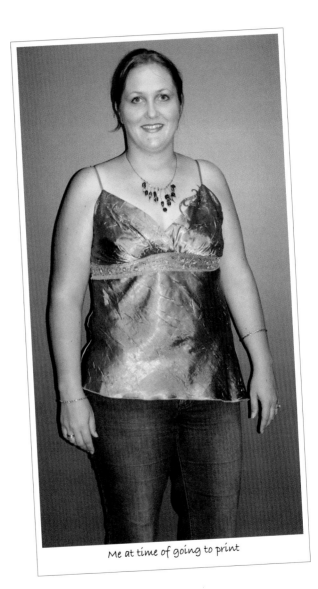

Me at time of going to print

DAY ONE HUNDRED AND SIXTY FOUR

I have been too busy to exercise lately so I have stayed at 84.6kgs.

My brother had his Buck's night last night (yes two days before his wedding). His lovely friends decided to get him completely drunk and send him into town dressed as a Genie. Consequently he found himself in hospital this morning with severe head injuries.

Why do men have to be so macho?

I am not sure exactly what happened but it seems he was up against three or four guys kicking him in the head… How does this happen??? I cannot understand how human beings can behave like this, it makes me sick to think that there is enough tragedy in this world already, why make more?

Anyway the doctors think he will make a full recovery, but they are worried about the small bleed on his brain. His wedding is not going to go ahead, and his fiancé has spent the day ringing people to cancel. I feel so sorry for her as it was meant to be their big day. I am sure they will still get married when he is well, but it must be so disappointing!!!

I am going to go and visit him before Jen's wedding tonight I hope he is OK!

DAY ONE HUNDRED AND SIXTY FIVE

Oh my god…Jen's wedding was great! I was shitting myself about doing the reading, but it went well. I was still very worried about my brother, but the alcohol made me feel better. Yes, tequila makes you feel lovely!!! Jai reckons I had six or seven tequila sunrises, not to mention all the glasses of champagne.

I wore the size fourteen dress and I felt awesome! I know I still appear overweight but it feels different….more healthy. Lots of people commented on how nice I looked, especially the hair! I really did feel much more comfortable with everyone, almost as if I had become one of the gang again…a great feeling!!!

At the hospital Ben was quite unresponsive, but the doctors say it is to be expected, he has a very bad headache and they can't give him any strong pain relief. The poor guy! So it seems I have a few more weeks before my brother's wedding, a good excuse for losing more weight.

I just hope my worrying doesn't lead me astray, I have already had half a packet of chocolate biscuits tonight.…

DAY ONE HUNDRED AND SIXTY SEVEN

Firstly, Ben seems much better today. He was talking and eating for the first time, and the doctors are happy with his progress!

Secondly, I am completely losing control again… I weighed 84.8kgs this morning and have eaten badly today. I really cannot use my brother's illness as an excuse to get fat again!

Thirdly, my little boy starts Kindy tomorrow. I can't believe it! He is growing up so fast; next thing I know he will be bringing home girls and getting into fights…that is sooooooo scary. Well if he is still sleeping in my bed when he is fifteen I probably won't have to worry!!! Maybe he will just live with me forever.

No! I always said I wouldn't be the type of mother who thinks that no woman is good enough for her perfect little boy. I feel sorry for her already!!!

DAY ONE HUNDRED AND SIXTY EIGHT

I have exactly two weeks left until the end of my book. Don't worry I don't plan to stop losing weight at that point but I have to stick to my deadline. I am slightly behind in my goal of 69kgs, but hey you can't be disappointed with ten kilos right.

So far I have had a great time losing my weight and have tried not to let it consume me. I have definitely changed my lifestyle…I will never again doubt that you don't need to exercise to lose weight. And I would probably miss it if I stopped anyway!

Ok, I am still bingeing, but a lot less frequently, and when I do I have learnt to binge with normal food. And have saved a shit load of money by not eating so much take-away food. I have gone from having take-away three or four times a week to having it twice a fortnight. My serves are smaller now and chocolate no longer lives next to the bed.

I haven't tried too many new foods, but I did have pineapple on Christmas day and prawns a few weeks ago. I will keep trying…

DAY ONE HUNDRED AND SIXTY NINE

I feel disgusting this morning…

Last night I came home from the hospital late so we got fish and chips for tea. God, it was gross! I won't do that again for a long time, I feel as though my body is coated in margarine. How disappointing. A good lesson though!

To top it all off…today I got home from the hospital to find the remnants of World War three. The boys had played with almost every toy they own, and their daddy had clearly spent the majority of his time watching the cricket. This makes me soooooooooo angry! I just get so frustrated.

I don't understand how men can lay comfortably on the sofa whilst the rest of the house goes down the drain. I can't even go to bed at night unless the house is reasonably tidy.

Now this has taken me about five years to grasp, but here it is, the truth about men… they don't care about the mess… It's simple they just don't care. So when you get home, walk through the door and straight to the vacuum cleaner and spend the next hour vacuuming aggressively (as though you want to kill someone), don't expect a thank you... it isn't happening. Ladies, the truth is you are not vacuuming for him; you are doing it for yourself, you are the one who likes it clean! Don't be pissed off, it's a waste of energy. They just don't care!!! Trust me he would be much more grateful if you got naked and served him beer whilst you bathed in the trash together.

So the advice is simple, don't get angry when you find yourself picking up after him, you are wasting your own sanity. And secondly, if they are lazy before you get married, then they will be lazy after the wedding. Don't fool yourself – he won't change. If you want him to help around the house more, just find something that he likes doing and give him that job. Jai likes doing the washing, so when he's home from work he gets to do it all. That way I don't get pissed off every night when I do everything else.

It is my birthday tomorrow, lets see if he can redeem himself...

DAY ONE HUNDRED AND SEVENTY

Happy Birthday to me, happy birthday to me, happy birthday to meeeeeeeeee. Gosh I am kidding myself; I really used to love my birthday. Now that I am a grown up it has lost its excitement. Why can't I be ten again?

So today I went with my mum, aunty and sister, out for lunch and a movie. We saw a movie called Closer. Well I am sure the oldies in the back row were not wishing they were closer, or maybe it made them realise how close to death they really are. The movie was slightly more graphic and rude than we had expected. It was nice to watch Jude Law though he's a real hotty! When is he going to do a movie with Brad Pitt??? That would be a great duo, maybe he could join them for Ocean's Thirteen…Gosh I need a cold shower!!!

I only ate one eighth of my popcorn and didn't do too badly at lunch. But remember…its my birthday and I can binge if I want to!!!

Jai gave me a Rubik's cube for my birthday, and before you say anything, yes I did ask for it. One of those things I always wanted as a child, everyone else had one!!! He says he can't give me my proper present today because it takes time to organise. Well that's a bloody cop out… I want my present!!!

"I want the world. I want the whole world. I want to lock it all up in my pocket. It's my bar of chocolate. Give it to me now"[23]. Don't worry, I'm not as bad as Veruca Salt, I can wait…

DAY ONE HUNDRED
AND SEVENTY ONE

Still no present?

Luckily I had thought ahead and bought myself a night at the very luxurious Burswood Resort Casino, I decided that since we had the money I deserve a night away from everything. Yes I am staying by myself!!!

I can't wait…

DAY ONE HUNDRED
AND SEVENTY TWO

I am such a bitch…I spent the whole day yesterday drilling Jai about my birthday present. I just couldn't understand why he hadn't given me anything yet. This is the first year that he has actually had money, so why no present? I kept on begging him to give it to me, but he wouldn't, he said it was a surprise. He told me to be patient… What the hell??? I am an Aquarian.

So I was forced to wait.

Then when I checked into my hotel room, I got the shock of my life. Jai had arranged a basket of flowers, chocolates, cashews and champagne to be waiting for me in my room. Oh my god… I have the best husband in the universe!!! I was so overwhelmed that I burst into tears, it was the nicest thing anyone has ever done for me.

I had a great night… I met friends in the evening, and then slept all night. I had such a good sleep; it was so good that I woke up with a sore bum from not moving all night. I just love those hotel sheets!!! And guess what they even have scales in the rooms, and they must be rigged lighter! Yay, no guilt!!!

My sister came up to my room for breakfast; we had

pancakes, croissants and toast, yes a carbohydrate feast, and a delicious one at that!! We then gambled for a few hours, had a relaxing neck and shoulder massage and went on to visit Ben in the hospital. He is doing well.

But the best part came when I got home... My wonderful husband had cleaned the whole house it looked immaculate. Boy is he going to get some good sex tonight!

DAY ONE HUNDRED AND SEVENTY FOUR

Big Day Out

Boy was it a Big Day Out… what can I say, perhaps I am getting tooooo old for that sort of thing. When I turned twenty-one I had a party the night before the Big Day Out, now I have to have a big night in just to prepare!

I had a great day though, I saw the Beastie Boys for the first time. They were awesome, and you know what – they are also much older than me. I spent most of the day catching up with friends and even got trapped in the Grinspoon mosh pit. A memorable experience!

But the best part of the day came when Jai's friend Anthony told me that I looked very 'healthy'. He later (when he was sloshed) went on to say that he meant I had lost heaps of weight but didn't think he should say it, in fear of hurting my feelings. Sorry boys I am over hurt feelings, just say it!!! I did look much better, and I felt so too.

I saw a few friends from high school there and rather than dodge them I decided to just bite the bullet and say hello. I am glad I did.

DAY ONE HUNDRED
AND SEVENTY FIVE

This morning we got a call from the police asking family members to be part of a press conference to call out for witnesses to Ben's attack. Oh my god, I am going to be on TV!!!

Well no I wasn't going to be on TV, they apparently didn't need me…So I went along for support. When we got there, they shuffled us into the studio and told me to sit up front.… what??? I thought I wasn't needed, crap I didn't put on makeup…how can this be fair. I was then sat next to my very beautiful, size six sister-in-law-to-be, and the whole of WA was about to see it.

Don't worry though they only showed me on channel Ten, and Jai reckons it looked like I was about to flash my boobs, maybe I should have pulled a Janet Jackson, it would have been great publicity for my book. Anyway, they published a photo of My Dad, Ben's fiancé and me in the West Australian. Of course they had to print us on the colour page to more adequately show the pink in Ben's genie outfit.

So far no calls from modelling agencies… maybe it will take a day or two.

DAY ONE HUNDRED
AND SEVENTY EIGHT

Well this book is meant to be about weight loss and I have gone off track a bit lately. So here goes I weighed 84.4kgs this morning and I am very happy about it. I plan to get back into the cross training this week. Hopefully life will get back to normal soon.

Ben came home from hospital today. He is much better!

DAY ONE HUNDRED AND EIGHTY

I just realised I am near to the end and I still haven't researched the brown bread vs white bread thing, so here goes:

Dr Trisha Macnair states that:

"Bread of any type is a healthy food because it is high in complex carbohydrates and low in fat and sugar (but be careful what you put on the bread!). It's also a good source of iron and calcium."[24]

She also states that:

"The extra health benefits of brown bread come from the wheat grains which make brown bread brown. Whole-wheat grain is a good source of fibre, protein and B vitamins. In white bread the husk of the grain is removed and only the inner part of the grain is used." [24]

Come on we all know that, what about the weight gain thing? Sorry no answer, there doesn't seem to be anything about it on the internet. I think I will keep eating brown bread though…

Well whilst I didn't find any more interesting information relating to bread, I did find this article:

Mental health: You are what you eat[25]

The article outlines the correlation between food and mood, they refer to a published book written by nutritional therapist Amanda Geary. The "Mind Guide to Food and Mood" lists some of the foods that are most likely to affect people's moods including:

- *artificial flavourings and preservatives*
- *chocolate*
- *coffee*
- *eggs*
- *milk products*
- *oranges*
- *sugar*
- *wheat products.*

"Foods required for good mental health include plenty of fruit and vegetables and those containing essential fatty acids, such as sardines, tuna, salmon, pumpkin and walnuts"[25].

I am screwed!!!

DAY ONE HUNDRED AND EIGHTY ONE

I started my job at the hospital today and wow I am buggered. I haven't worked for nearly a year and you can tell. I have a blister on my heel and am in dire need of a foot massage. I managed to shower a few patients and help them with breakfast. The one thing I hadn't expected to be doing was extracting teeth.

What a bad nurse… after his shower I asked my patient to do his teeth, I was away from him for only a few seconds and when I came back his whole face was covered in blood. Oh my god!!! He then passed me one of his teeth. I could not believe my eyes. He had been trying to get his partial dentures out for cleaning (they were already in a container by the sink) and accidentally removed one of his real teeth. I am glad he was not in any pain… a great first day!

Since I am one day away from completing this book I thought I had better measure myself again. Here are my final measurements (cms):

Body area	30 May 2004	14 Feb 2005	Loss
Neck	39	36.5	2.5
Chest	106	101	5
Waist	109	102	7
Hips	120	114	6
Thigh	63	58	5
Calf	40	39	1
Arm	38	32	6

Wow!!! That really does put it into perspective… a total loss of 32.5 centimetres!

Yes it is Valentine's Day, and no I don't expect any romance. Jai and I decided six years ago to boycott this occasion, simply because we were broke. I will not be disappointed if I don't get anything, I am still buzzing from my birthday!

DAY ONE HUNDRED
AND EIGHTY TWO

I cannot believe this is my final entry. When I started this journey I was so far from the finish I never imagined completing it. I may not have lost the twenty-five kilos I set out to lose. But today I am ten kilos lighter than I was six months ago; I never truly believed that I could even lose five, so I am stoked.

The reality is there were three changes that, combined, resulted in my weight loss:

Increased water intake It does feel good to be hydrated, in the last six months I have had less headaches than ever before, I am sure this is the reason.

Exercising 30 minutes per day Another obvious one. All I can say is that it is bloody hard to start, but once you have it's not that bad.

Eating well Yes, it's true – the less fatty food you eat the more energy you have.

Ok, so anyone who has ever been to Weight Watchers knows this, so what is so special about my journey? I did it myself… I believed in myself, I did it for me and you know what… I am so proud of myself. I just want to scream to the world "you can lose weight, it is not a myth". I have taught myself that every excuse I have ever used to avoid losing weight, is just a cop-out… what is that saying… "I once was weak but now am strong" something like that.

You know what though, I am genuinely sad today… I feel as if I am saying goodbye to you all. A bit strange really, considering you probably won't read this for a few years. I thank you anyway for being my motivation, and hope that you can be successful too. I know that this journey has changed me in many ways and I guarantee I will continue on my path to thinness, until my goal is met.

So people, I am your proof! There is no excuse not to lose weight, the next time you are disheartened by a commercial where the person says "I lost 52 kilos in 16 weeks", just think of me. I lost ten kilos in six months, and you know what… I have never felt better!

Goodbye and Good luck…

See you on the beach!!!

THE END

UPDATE

Well here I am two months later, and I must confess… I have sinned, only slightly, but overall I am still on track. I have lost a couple more kilos, and weighed in this morning at 81.6kgs. I feel great! I even have the confidence to make eye contact with people at the shops now; it's amazing how many smiles you can get from people if you actually look at them. I have had so many compliments lately, on the first day back at uni one lady called me the "amazing shrinking woman", wow!!

I believe that the key to long-term weight loss is accountability. It's the coming to grips with the reality of nutrition and exercise, and throwing all those old excuses away that gives you the power to succeed. Don't give up… remember if you take two steps forward and one step back, you are still ahead!

Don't forget your local doctor is a great weight loss advisor. He or she can give you correct nutritional information and monitor your weight loss correctly. They can even help you to manage your psychological eating issues. Go on what do you have to lose??? Except a few kilos… and all your fat clothes…

I thank you for reading my story; I hope you found it motivating. If you have any questions for me, or weight loss stories you would like to share with me I would love to hear from you, please contact me as below, and keep a look out for my e-magazine coming soon on my web site:

Internet: goodfriendsbringsalad.com.au

Email: contactus@goodfriendsbringsalad.com.au

Mail: PO Box 905
Joondalup 6919
Western Australia

"Thou shouldst eat to live; not live to eat."
Socrates (469BC-399BC)

PERSONAL RECORD – MEASUREMENTS

Body area	Start Date	Finish Date
Neck		
Chest		
Waist		
Hips		
Thigh		
Calf		
Arm		

PERSONAL RECORD –WEIGHT

Date	Weight	Difference

ACKNOWLEDGEMENTS

I would like to thank my sister Toni for being supportive of my dream. Toni was the first person to read the book and the first to give me feedback; she truly motivated my writing and my weight loss. Thanks Toni xoxox

I would also like to thank Sandra, my mother in law, who was my proofreader and in many ways my inspiration. I am so grateful to have such a caring mother in law.

To my very talented Dad you are an amazing writer. I thank you for your encouragement, I am so proud of you… xoxox

My wonderful husband Jai, thank you for being so supportive and for allowing me to share our lives with the rest of the world… I love you, sexy bum…

I must thank the SSS for being a great source of fun and friendship over the past ten years… Especially Emma and Marcia for their feedback and support you guys rock!

I thank Leigh for her hard work on the design and for so willingly helping me bring this all together… You are a gem!

And finally I would like to thank Jeff Martin for giving me the passion to get up off my butt and make something of myself, your music is an inspiration to us all…

REFERENCES

1 The University of Sydney. (August 2004).
  What is the Glycemic Index?
  Retrieved August 11, 2004, from
  http://www.glycemicindex.com/

2 Australian Consumer's Association. (March 2004).
  Glyceamic Index… what's it all about?
  Retrieved November 24, 2004, from
  http://www.choice.com.au/viewArticle.aspx?id=1042
  25&catId=100289&tid=100008&p=5

3 World Health Organization. (2003).
  Obesity and Overweight: fact sheet.
  Retrieved August 15, 2004, from
  http://www.who.int/hpr/NPH/docs/gs_obesity.pdf

4 Better Health Channel. (December 1999).
  Healthy Eating for Children and Adults.
  Retrieved February 19, 2005, from
  http://www.betterhealth.vic.gov.au/bhcv2/bhcarticles.
  nsf/pages/Healthy_eating_for_children_and_adults?
  OpenDocument

5 Woolworths. (2004).
  Food Labels.
  Retrieved August 17, 2004, from
  http://www.woolworths.com.au/dietinfo/rsa8.asp

6 Heart Foundation. (2004).
  He*art Disease Facts.*
  Retrieved January 1, 2005, from
  http://www.heartfoundation.com.au/index.cfm?page=47

7 *Super size me* [Film]. (2004).
Spurlock, M. Samuel Goldwyn films.
Web Address
http://www.supersizeme.com/home.aspx

8 McCann, S. (2004).
What is food addiction?
Retrieved November 22, 2004, from
http://www.anonymityone.com/faq195.htm

9 Anonymous. (2003).
Junk food junkies. Better Nutrition. Vol. 65, Iss.10; p. 28

10 Newcombe, R. (2003).
Is junk food addictive?
Retrieved November 22, 2004, from
http://www.bupa.co.uk/health_information/html/hea
lth_news/190703 addic.html

11 Dr. Mezmer's World of Bad Psychology. (2004).
Addiction.
Retrieved November 24, 2004, from
http://www.homestead.com/flowstate/ daddiction.html

12 Addiction Intervention Resources. (2004).
Food Addiction.
Retrieved November 24, 2004, from
http://www.addictionintervention.com/ FoodAddiction.asp

13 CNN.com/health. (2003).
Diet guru Dr. Robert Atkins dead at 72.
Retrieved November 27, 2004, from
http://www.cnn.com/2003/HEALTH /04/17 /obit .atkins/

14 Diet Information. (2004).
Atkins diet review.
Retrieved November 27, 2004, from
http://www.dieti.com/diets/atkins-diet.htm

15 Sims, J. (2004).
   Atkins - the unhealthy choice.
   Retrieved November 27, 2004, from
   http://www.weightlossresources.co.uk/diet/atkins_
   diet/medical_ report.htm

16 Gastric Bypass Treatment.com. (2004).
   Surgical weight loss procedures.
   Retrieved December 4, 2004, from
   http://www.gastric-bypass-treatment.com/
   surgicalweight-loss-procedures.aspx

17 Australian Bureau of Statistics. (1997).
   National Survey of Mental Health and Well Being.
   Retrieved December 5, 2004, from
   http://www.mhca.com.au/Public/AboutMentalHealth/
   Statistics.html

18 Australian Institute of Health and Welfare. (2004).
   Mental Health Services in Australia 2001-02.
   Retrieved December 5, 2004, from
   http://www.aihw.gov.au/publications/hse/mhsa01-
   02/mhsa01-02-040719.pdf

19 National Institute of Mental Health. (2001). Eating
   Disorders: Facts About Eating Disorders and the
   Search for Solutions.
   Retrieved December 19, 2004, from
   http://www.nimh.nih.gov/publicat/
   eatingdisorders.cfm#ed3

20 Australian Institute of Health and Welfare. (2001).
Cancer in Australia 2001.
Retrieved January 11, 2005, from
http://www.aihw.gov.au/publications/can/ca01/ca01.pdf

21 McCoy, R. (2001).
Breast self-examination: Looking after yourself.
Retrieved January 11, 2005, from
http://www.healthnetwork.com.au/searchdisplay.ph
p?cat=tests&id=11

22 Rondel, P. (2005).
TV promises.

23 Dahl, R. (1964).
Charlie and the chocolate factory.
Retrieved February 20, 2005, from
http://www.garnersclassics.com/qwonka.htm

24 Macnair, T. (2000).
Brown bread vs white bread.
Retrieved February 13, 2005, from
http://www.bbc.co.uk/health/ask_doctor/bread.shtml

25 BBC news. (2000).
Mental health: You are what you eat.
Retrieved February 13, 2005, from
http://news.bbc.co.uk/1/hi/health/1021676.stm